CHIEFS, PAWNS & WARRIORS

A MEMOIR OF FIREFIGHTER RON PARKER'S 9/11 EXPERIENCE

Ron Parker

Ron Parker & Associates
P.O. Box 1332
Boynton Beach, FL 33425-1332
www.AuthorRonParker.com

Ordering Information:
Quantity Sales. Special discounts are available on quantity purchases by corporations, associations, and others. For details, contact the publisher at the address above.

Printed in the United States of America
Second Printing, 2014

To my brothers who walked with me to hell and back, and to those who lost their way on the return home-I humbly dedicate this book.

CONTENTS

ACKNOWLEDGEMENTS

I would first like to thank my wife, Judy, for assisting me in completing the very difficult task of writing this book. You put up with all of my misgivings and demands for instant perfection with incredible grace without faulting me for my floundered thoughts and words. There aren't enough flowers or thankful gestures that I could lovingly give you to correct my ridiculous meltdowns, rants and raves, and endless wrong doings. Your love for me has never been stronger and I appreciate that agape love. I am more grateful than ever to have you as my soulmate.

As for my two sons, Jonathan and Blaze, thank you for allowing me to do my thing and never making me feel bad for dedicating time to write.

As for Diesel, my dog and faithful companion, who stayed up late beside me guarding my words and my being, you're the best dog anyone could have.

I would also like to thank my very dear friends who also made this book possible, Richard and Ilene Patasnik (especially Ilene who helped me enormously from the very beginning with the help of her daughter Jerri), my number one fan Uncle Buddy Rodney, Edie and Richard Feinstein, Irene and Richard Weinstein, and Stan Weisleder.

To all the people who supported me along the way-Mike and Debbie Kevlin, Linda Grillo and her beautiful daughters Jessica and Corinne, Peter and Lori Ferrara, Cousin John, Kevin McFeely, Cousin Ivan, Jim Falcone, Tim Duffy, Mickey Kross, Kimberly Greiger, Beverly and Richard Stapf, Jr., Donna Mcquire, Lillian and Fred Raymond, Palm Beach Captain Matt viii

Willhite, Brett Hill, Robert Calise, Kathy Bien, George Johnson, Danny O'Donavan and my artist friend Chris Pontello-I thank you all so much and I couldn't have done it without you.

Thank you to my old friends from Brooklyn, Lenny and Dawn Colletto, Sandy and Mick Goddard and Lance Marz.

I would also like to thank the following individuals who also went above and beyond to see this book come to life: Karen Ellis, Robert Casaburi, John Lapi, Ivan Marcano, Joe McCloskey, Mary E. Thompson and Briana Ulrich.

To the dozens of others who were part of the process of producing this book and are not named here, thank you, thank you, thank you! Know that your support is not forgotten and your sacrifices have not been in vain.

Never forgetting and always loving my mom, Nancy Parker.

INTRODUCTION

E veryone remembers where they were and what they were doing the moment they heard about September 11, 2001. For those who were in New York at the time, it started as the first day back to school for our children. It was a day for us to exercise our democratic right to vote in the primary. It was a bright, sunny, clear and cool fall day that invited you to go outside. But 8:46 am brought a downward spiral into a horrible, terrible, nightmarish day that changed many of our lives forever. As horrible as it was, it is my challenge to you to never forget that day or the lessons that it holds for each of us.

Before I begin talking more about what we can learn from the destruction of the World Trade Center, I want to talk with you about its history. It was a neighborhood in New York, just like many other city neighborhoods such as China Town, Little Italy and Times Square. This 16 acre site was known as "Radio Row." It was a small community of a few thousand people who were either ham radio operators or home TV repairmen. People from all over the city would come to buy parts-such as tubes, diodes, cathodes and even transistors to fix their radios and TVs. Yes, believe it or not, tubes and transistors were used long before microchips or personal computers were even contemplated! The community didn't want their neighborhood as they knew it abolished and destroyed to make way for the World Trade Center. They eventually lost their case in court. They referred to the towers as, "the box the empire state building came in."

1

The World Trade Center was not just the two towers, but a compilation of 7 buildings. Its foundation was a 75 foot reverse bathtub that dug into the bedrock to keep the Hudson River from seeping into the site-a first-time engineering feat. Japanese architect Minoru Yamasaki, who was deathly afraid of heights, specifically created a design of columns, just 22 inches wide between the windows, so you could lean out and press against the side of the columns while you looked out the windows. The columns were designed to provide a sense of security.

The towers themselves somehow seemed to be alive. Although there was enough concrete in the World Trade Center towers to produce a 5 foot walkway from NYC to Washington DC, the towers were flexible enough to sway one to three feet in each direction when the wind blew. On the upper floors, such as in the "Windows of the World" restaurant on the top floor, you could look down at what seemed to be ants. The sun would shine upon you while the ants on the ground would open up their umbrellas to take cover from the rain falling from clouds that were below where you were standing. If you looked out straight ahead on a clear day you could see up to 50 miles away with the naked eye. The swaying took a bit of getting used to and it wasn't uncommon to see the glass windows ripple and spill or to see aircrafts flying well below where you were sitting.

In addition to the 40,000 people who worked at the Trade Center, another 250,000 people would traverse there every day connecting on the PATH trains from New Jersey and the main artery of the NYC transit hub. The mall was under the site. With 11.2 million square feet of space, the World Trade Center had its own zipcode-10048. The World Trade Center *was the place to be* in NYC. The right to claim the World Trade Center as a place of employment inspired envy. Most people don't have a workplace that is a city within the city-live music and entertainment was common place in the outdoor mall. And besides its architectural innovations, the towers had other claims to fame. Believe it or not, a French guy named Philippe Petit actually tight roped across the buildings in 1974. California high-rise rescue firefighter Dan Goodwin successfully scaled the North Tower to advocate the possibility of rescue in high-rise buildings.

Now that you know more about what life was like before the World Trade Center was built and what life was like once they became part of the NYC experience, you may be wondering what there is left to learn from by its destruction on 9/11 and why it should be remembered. Although there were previous attempted bombings on the World Trade Center, an attack of this scale that could demolish two 110 story buildings was considered impossible. The building's freight elevator was the fastest in the world and it could carry passengers and other service items from the ground floor to the top in one minute. But once the integrity of the structures were compromised, it took less than 10 seconds for each of the 110 story towers to collapse into 20 stories of twisted, mangled steel, debris and clouds of smoke, cement, ash and papers that spread well beyond the 16 acre site. The steel girders that once supported the iconic buildings now looked like a huge pile of twisted pick-up-sticks.

I remember St. Paul's Church, just across the street from Church and Fulton Street. Its wooden roof and stained glass window accented building was built in 1765. While the New Millennium Hotel, with all its shattered glass windows, was on fire right across the street from the church and the trees in the church's graveyard were burning, God protected that church-not a single pane of stained glass or a shingle was damaged.

Historically, St. Paul's was one of the first churches in New York City. President George Washington had his own private box and pew in there. I remember the church transformed into a calm, restful, and soulful place of peace and tranquility for emergency personnel. The church had neat rows of cots covered with homemade quilts and blankets. There was also a teddy bear on each pillow. I couldn't believe that such a beautiful quiet oasis as this was just a few feet away from the unimaginable hell and destruction surrounding me. While I was in the church I selected a seat in George Washington's private pew. God had a purpose for that church that I don't claim to understand, but I know how they helped me cope during that difficult time.

Children from all over the world sent cards and letters by the sacks to the church so that they could be given out to the first responders who sought refuge there. I even received Christmas cards and ornaments from one of the shipments. Every Christmas I still hang a shell with a pearl on my tree that came from the people of the New Orleans 9th Ward as a Christmas gift. Each year that I hang the ornament I think of their own suffering during the aftermath of hurricane Katrina and I pray that they're all well.

I often think about the Pearl Harbor Memorial where the *USS Arizona* rests. If you are fortunate enough to visit, you may have the opportunity to meet one of the 2,400 sailors who served on the battleship in Pearl Harbor on December 7, 1941. He could be as old as 88 at the time of this writing, but he would gladly share with you his personal account of the surprise attack on his ship. If you are a history buff, you may think you know the story. But when he tells you what happened in his own words from his own perspective, the same way he had probably told that story for 72 years, you will be experiencing the priceless opportunity to relive it with him before his lips are sealed forever. He didn't ask to be a part of it, but he spoke up nevertheless.

I believe that patriots who lived through history, like the sailors who lived through Pearl Harbor, have passed the torch to me to continue the legacy of sharing the history of our great land. It is not something I have asked for, but in honor of the first responders who cannot be here to tell their story, I gladly accept the responsibility of sharing about how they lived in their final moments. I try to cherish each day that I am alive and I thank God for everything He has given me.

Just as an attack of the magnitude of what happened at Ground Zero was thought to be impossible, many of us have impossible tragedies that occur in our lives. It can be losing a loved one who kept the family together, it could be a divorce from what you thought was the perfect marriage, it could be a personal attack on your life or the person who robbed you of your confidence or sense of safety. It can be anything. But the stories that unfold in the pages to follow are the stories of a nation that has been knocked down but refuses to stay down. They are the stories of a city that has been physically dismantled while its heart for its people only grows stronger. They are the stories of a man who relied on his training, his brotherhood of firefighters and faith in God to carry him through the darkest of nights. They are the stories that are recorded with the hope that they inspire to face the very things that cause you pain and begin to live a life that "Never Forgets" the past while still building towards the future.

On that fateful day the City of New York suffered 2,753 terrorist related deaths (not including any of the high jackers). Of the 2,753, American Airlines Flight Number 11 accounted for 87 deaths and United Airlines Flight Number 175 accounted for another 60. First responders accounted for 411, or 15% of the total, broken down as follows: 343 from the NY Fire Department, 37 from the NY Port Authority, 23 from the NY Police Department and 8 EMT's. The NY Fire Department losses of 343 made up 12 1/2 % of the total losses and included 1 Chaplain and 2 Paramedics. As of 9-11-13, only 1,637 of the victims have been identified, leaving 1,116 unidentified or worse yet, unaccounted for.

CHAPTER ONE

Brave Heart

I wave hello to my favorite bartender, Conner, as I hurriedly enter my favorite watering hole and squeeze past the crowded bar to join my friends. The Jackal is a nondescript little joint nestled between the giant towers that comprise the World Trade Center on Hudson Street. As I breeze by, Conner muffles something about how I owe him because his Red Sox pummeled my beloved Yankees last week. I was already late to catch up with my friends, so I nodded in acknowledgement in hopes that he wouldn't give me too hard of a time about it tonight.

My dear friends were in the back nestled around a small round table overloaded with beer and other libations. I could tell that they had started the party without the honored guest-which was me.

It's an unbelievable feeling to know that all of my friends and fellow colleagues, even the ones I have not seen for months, put together this little gala event just for me. It seemed so miniscule in regards to the overflowing number of patrons at the bar, but it still meant the world to me. Besides, we are all tech-geeks not trendy elaborate party planners and trendsetters. They were sincerely proud of me for being the first to be promoted.

"Cheers! Cheers!" resounded over and over in our small corner. Collectively, we have worked for years to modify, perfect and incorporate a far advanced computerized system that would turn Wall Street on its head by impacting Forex trading market like never before. Forex is the largest market in the world and trades nearly $2 trillion worth of currency each day. That currency represents all of the currency in the world and my promotion was going to allow me to change the way it all happens. Cantor Fitzgerald, the investment bank that hired me, didn't quite understand my system or how it would benefit them but they understood enough to recognize that hiring me and giving me free reign to use my system to take Cantor Fitzgerald to new heights as an industry innovator. Their new slogan said it all, "The engine of the new market." I was so confident and eager to employ my new trading system.

After a few hours of drinking, my colleagues presented me with a gift that was cleverly wrapped in yellow caution tape, the kind you see used by police and firefighters to cordon off areas of danger. As I struggled to remove the over wrapped package I realize they had gotten me the greatest gag gift anyone could ever give to me. They knew me all too well. They knew that my acceptance of Cantor's offer requires me to leave my old company on the 5th floor of 77 Water St. and move to a corner office with floor-to-ceiling glass walls on the 105th floor of the North Tower. They knew that I was deathly afraid of heights. And amidst a tumultuous roar from my crowd of friends, I lifted my newly acquired prize-a parachute.

I couldn't believe my eyes. It was a real parachute, not your basic military white one. It was a professional state-of-the-art base jumping model that deployed a bright red canopy. Embroidered on the strap was my new nickname "Brave Heart." We all laughed until our sides ached.

I started my new job at Cantor on Monday, September 10, 2001. I was treated like royalty. As soon as I stepped off the elevator on the 105th floor I was greeted by most of the senior partners as well as my new staff and personal secretary. They led me into this beautiful corner office with astounding endless views, the only problem was that I stopped at the threshold of the door way and had great difficulty proceeding forward into my own office. My abrupt stop caused the entourage that closely followed me to bump into each other in the process. I imagine that the look on my face gave away the cause for my sudden stop as I stared at the two walls of glass facing the city of New York, because suddenly everyone had a meeting to attend that they just remembered. Only Gladys, my personal secretary, stayed by my side as I blinked several times and began silently telling myself "I'm ok. I'm ok."

In an effort to recover from the doorway mishap, I took a deep breath and stared at my feet as I gingerly took one step at a time towards my new chair. After settling in at my desk, I was glad to see that the beautiful leather chair was facing inward towards the rest of the office.

As Gladys offered me soda and juice from the coffee-less coffee room and warned me about the homemade donuts from a co-worker with misguided aspirations of moonlighting as Betty Crocker, I scanned the office and admired its beautiful and apparently expensive artwork on the walls that tastefully framed the oversized and extensively ornate desk. As my eyes settled on a door to my right, Gladys, explained that it was a private executive bathroom complete with shower. I declined her invitation to look at it myself because my heartbeat was just starting to slow down as I recovered from my first glimpse of the two walls of windows that showed just how high 105 stories really is. I didn't want to find out how I would react if I had to look at it again on the walk back to my seat from the executive bathroom. I simply took her word that it existed and suspected that it would be just as nice as the office.

I couldn't help but notice the new company mouse pad that was designed specifically for my arrival, which read "Cantor Fitzgerald. The engine of the new market." Gladys informed me that my personal belongings would be delivered promptly for me to arrange in my cavernous office. Shortly thereafter a box was delivered to my office. It was filled with personal photographs of my family. Both of my parents and Rex, a French bulldog, were in every photograph. Mom and Dad were especially proud of my accomplishments. I would like to think that Rex was proud too, but as long as he gets his treats on time when I get home in the afternoon I guess he doesn't really care where I've been working all day. As I peered down at the bottom of the box a sense of calm began to overtake me. At the very bottom of my box was my last remaining item-my personalized "Brave Heart" parachute.

A terrible rainy night released an unbelievably beautiful, clear and crisp morning that can only be described as the perfect day. This was the kind of day that I wish I could just bottle and spend playing Frisbee with Rex. But of course I couldn't skip out on my second day on the job with, of all companies, Cantor Fitzgerald!

At 7:15 am on September 11, 2001, I paused briefly in front of the gigantic glass structure, looking up to see if I could locate my corner office on the hundred and fifth floor. I'm not sure what made me stop, but when you come to work this early, why not? Although there are only four corners to the building, I really couldn't be certain which corner surrounded my office because I hadn't looked out at all the previous day to even see which direction my office faced. I immersed myself in unlocking and unleashing my new system. I did not remove my eyes from my computer screen to even glance outside that previous day.

It was now 8:46 AM and suddenly I became a hemorrhage of the glass tower as I clung to the legs of my desk that hung perilously outside the window of my 105th story window. I hung there dazed and confused as my mind instantly replayed how my super padded high-back chair slammed through the impregnable window designed to withstand gale force hurricane winds as well as the forced strain and twisting that characterized the normal swaying of the

superstructure. After shattering the glass, the chair was ejected from the building while I managed to cling to the leg of my oversized desk that was only inches from falling into the abyss.

I finally convinced myself to loosen my death grip on the leg of the colossal desk long enough to crawl back inside the building before the blunt force trauma to my head caused me to pass out. I came to coughing and vomiting in total darkness with wet blood covering my head. Due to the high heat and deadly smoke that encompassed everything around me, I was barely cognizant and could not understand what had happened or how long I had been lying on the floor of that now completely destroyed office. I felt as if every bone in my body was broken and the intensity of the pain convinced me that I was still alive. I was scared and frightened beyond belief. This was exactly why I was afraid of heights!

Unbeknownst to me, the shattered window that once threatened my life actually helped spare my life by allowing the fresh air to seep intermittently into my office and keep me alive. Somehow my right hand remained on the leg of that desk throughout my ordeal. My other arm was laying over my miracle; that gag gift parachute with my name on it-Brave Heart.

There was nothing to think about. In a matter of seconds I donned that parachute like a well-seasoned professional skydiver-broken bones and all. But I was not quick enough. What I didn't know was that the shattered window allowing fresh air for my survival was also drawing the fiery devil of flames that seemed to start only two to six stories below my office. Craving the oxygen as fuel for consumption and growth, the flames enveloped my office with the unimaginable rapid intense heat from Hades itself, forcefully pushing me outside the 105 story building. Grasping the chute's release handle, I instinctively pulled it and immediately deployed a beautiful red fully enveloped canopy. At the precise moment of my miracle canopy opening, glass and steel debris from what appeared to be an explosion in the south tower pierced and slashed through my canopy and accelerating gravities pull on both me and what I had hoped to be my red fabric of hope.

Many weeks had passed at Ground Zero, now conveniently referred to as *The Pile*. I was now working in recovery mode, searching for lost souls painstakingly with a small handheld gardener's rake or fork. I snagged a small red fabric- a fabric unlike anything I had uncovered previously. As I yanked, pulled and unearthed it, the fabric grew larger and larger. Most recovered articles were mostly unrecognizable to the naked eye, but your mind plays tricks on you sometimes. Your concentration is super focused not to miss any small detail that will help you recover someone. Perhaps it was part of a set of fancy drapes or material to adorn one of the many decorated offices, possibly something from one of the shops of the underground mall. The super bright red fabric seem to have had nylon cords attached further discovering a harness with the words BRAVE HEART embroidered on it. Was it possible? Or was it my mind playing tricks on me. I was dumbfounded...a parachute? It was a freaking parachute! Although it was torn and burnt, I confirmed that it was a parachute as I gathered it up. As I freed the last bit of the parachute from *The Pile*, it unearthed something. There was a tattered mostly destroyed photo of a man playing Frisbee with a dog on a beautiful day. It looked like a French bulldog.

I jumped up as a trail of sweat tickled me as it meandered down the back of my neck. I quickly wiped it away as I quickly blinked three times and tried to take in the different parts of my surroundings. The red parachute and French bulldog picture was replaced with a large blue comforter that was draped over me. The longer I sat up the more I began to register the nightstand with the picture of my two boys, Jonathan and Blaze, my keys and wallet were on the dresser and the light was on in the bathroom as I heard sounds of running water for a shower.

I took a deep breath, exhaled and leaned back on the headboard as I realized that it was a nightmare. Everything from running into the bar, to getting the parachute gag gift, to being thrust out the side of the World Trade Center to finding the picture of the man with the Frisbee and French bulldog. Of course, it had to be a dream. *How could I be both the man who plunged to his death and the firefighter who found him?* How could a building that was built to survive hurricane force winds and designed to sway one to three feet actually snap like a toothpick and crumble to the ground. Crazy things happen in New York, but not things like that. It had to be a dream, right?

As I took another deep breath to calm myself down I noticed that familiar smell that every firefighter knows is the result of a night of tango in the flames. It was just then that I realized that I did have a nightmare, but all of it wasn't made up. The sharp twinge of pain shooting up the back of my legs confirmed that I had been in a terribly serious situation yesterday. As my feet hit the floor the details of the previous morning began to come back to me. Yesterday was Tuesday, September 11, 2001.

Tuesday, September 11, 2001

My morning routine always varies based on my work schedule. NY Firefighters work one of two tours: a 9 am to 6 pm tour we call a *9 by* or the 6 pm to 9 am tour we call the *6 by*. Everyone knows that regardless of what time your tour is set to start, you are supposed to arrive at least an hour earlier to relieve one of the firefighters who worked the previous shift. So on the days I work the 9 by I'll make sure to leave home no later than 6 am so I can beat the traffic and arrive at my Ladder 184 Staten Island firehouse by 8 am-that's two hours of travel time. If I'm working the 6 by I can always leave at 4 pm and still make it by 5 pm because all the real traffic is coming out instead of going in. But with this being about one week into my three week vacation, I slept in until around 7:15 in the morning.

Jonathan, age 12, and Blaze, age 10, were having their first day of school in a new school and I wanted to make sure that I got them there on time. I started their morning by making them breakfast. It was nothing fancy, but I did enjoy being able to cook for a normal family of four instead of a firehouse of 11 hungry men. I gave them compliments on their new school clothes and walked them down to their new school and then turned around to come right back to the house.

17 years with the FDNY trained me well for three weeks as a house-husband. In between runs, down at the firehouse, there is always some kind of committee work we had to do. You were either making up the beds, doing laundry, scrubbing shower stalls, shining floors, cleaning pots or cooking for the 11 people who were always in the firehouse each shift. Now that I was off, the committee work continued but in a new location.

Around March we moved into a new home in New Jersey. We must have visited my cousin and my parents in their New Jersey homes too much because my wife Judy desperately wanted to move there too. I didn't take her requests all that seriously until one night she mentioned that we had an appointment the next day to look at some homes with a realtor she had tracked down. Before I knew it, we spent the morning and afternoon looking at two or three homes and by that same evening we were signing paperwork for our new home. Within a few more months we successfully relocated the other two residents of our triplex Brooklyn home. I told the residents of the top floor not to worry about trying to pay me back for the past year or so, that they didn't pay any rent and that they could just leave. As for my mother-in-law, who lived in the middle level, we found her a nice place at the end of the block.

Moving sounds like a simple process, but once you start cleaning and packing up every single toothpick, old high school yearbook and old baby toy from your pre-teen aged boys and transporting it to a new location where you discover that 15% of the stuff you thought you had when you packed is now missing and that you now have a desperate need for items that you never needed before, it can become a several month long process. So now, a full 6 months after we moved into the new home, I was still getting things settled. I even turned down a couple of gigs with my moonlighting job as a limo driver to make sure I could make a dent in my list.

As I began to tackle the first item on my list, the phone rang. It was my younger brother Greg. Even with nine years between us, we have always been pretty close through the years. There are five of us in total who are living. Our younger sister, Loretta, was born when I was five and died when I was eight, leaving only my brothers Charlie, a year and a half my senior and Richie who was born when I was three. Gregory who was born later, around the time I was ten, and finally Craig came around the time I was twelve years old. Gregory lived over in Long Island and it wasn't too rare to hear from him. What was rare was the flat tone he used with me on the phone, "Put the TV on. Something's going on."

I put the TV on and I saw the line "breaking news" across the bottom of the screen as I looked at what appeared to be smoke coming out of the North Tower of the World Trade Center. In the top left corner of the screen was the word "live." For a moment I was wondering if this was a preview for a new movie about something terrible happening in New York, this seemed to be the season for those types of movies, but as I flipped through a couple more channels and saw the same exact footage I knew this was no movie preview. As the reality of the image settled in I watched the second plane hit the other 110 story building and I knew I was no longer on vacation.

I turned to my wife Judy and told her that I had to go and she immediately understood. By now she was a full time homemaker, but her 20 years with the American Red Cross made her familiar with the process of how cities deal with disasters.

As I have so many times before when I'm in the firehouse and we get a call for a *run*, I dropped what I was doing and ran to my vehicle- this time it was my car instead of the *rig*. The difference is that now that I'm leaving from home and I've been on vacation and didn't have my gear, I wasn't sure what I was supposed to do. Do I race out to the towers and jump in where I can? Do I go to my new Ladder 84 in Staten Island to get my gear, report for duty and go from there? Do I really want to delay getting to the World Trade Center where I know my old friends from the Brooklyn Ladder 148 were already suited up and on their way to what was sure to be one of the greatest disasters any living New York firefighter had ever seen? But even if I did go to Manhattan, what was I going to be able to offer with no gear, no tools, no orders and I was pretty sure that there was no place for me to park the car. I knew that I had to go Staten Island first.

While I was thinking through which direction I was to go into next, I was already in the car listening for breaking news updates on the radio and driving as fast as I could on the shoulder of the road with no regard whatsoever for speed limits. As long as there was room for my car to safely get down that median and I knew I still had control of the vehicle, I was going to drive. Between my experiences with driving a chase-truck in my pre-firefighter days and racing to the scene of accidents to get the job for my collision shop and then my training as a backup chauffeur who has years of experience with driving a rig that is about 8 feet wide and at least 24 feet long, I knew I had this four door sedan under control even at 80-90 mph speeds. I wasn't alone in that median either, the other vehicles must have been firefighters, police officers and other emergency personnel people because they were flying down the road with me while the other cars were pulling over to the opposite side of the road. This was a total recall of everyone who had anything to do with the safety of our city.

I decided to take The Outerbridge to Staten Island instead of the tunnel. As I approached the bridge, which allows you to look directly over the mouth of the Hudson River at the famous Manhattan skyline, I could see the towers flaming and smoking and resisting the pull of gravity as their supporting girders were being pushed and burned to their physical limits. Now I start driving even faster and start pushing 105 mph.

There is always at least one officer at the firehouse, always. In our house it was either one of the three lieutenants or the captain. On September 11th it was the captain and I was so glad that it was him. He had to be at least a 40 year veteran. He was a salty no nonsense guy. "Sign into the journal. Get your gear ready," he ordered as soon as he saw me.

Now anybody who walks in or out of a firehouse has to sign the journal so that there is a written record to account for all of the activity. So I sign "R. Parker RFD" (Ready for Duty) in red ink instead of blue. If this was my normal shift, then I would have signed in blue. But when anything out of the ordinary happens, it is signed in red. This was definitely a red kind of day. And as other firefighters arrived they did the same.

"You're a chauffeur?" I heard over my right shoulder as I was getting my gear ready.

"Yeah, I am," I confirmed, "I can drive a rig-Hook and Ladder."

"You can take a spare apparatus to the site, but wait for orders from the battalion, with guys coming in and finding what to do with them."

I got my first set of orders and they put me in the driver's seat at least until I get my next set of orders. At least my drive to the firehouse already had me warmed up for this next drive. I knew I wouldn't be driving a fire truck because our house didn't have one. Spare rigs were mainly located out of the borough. Besides, our house was more accustomed to responding to car accidents, slip and fall accidents and medical emergencies other than fires so we did not complain about not having the spare fire truck taking up space in our quarters.

From all the talk back and forth over the radio I gathered that all of the Brooklyn and Manhattan firehouses were already depleted of their staff, trucks and equipment. So this meant that not only were there dozens of firemen already on the scene, but there were five boroughs with unmanned firehouses in case there was another attack, house fire, or car accident somewhere else in those boroughs. This is not standard FDNY operating procedure. So I knew that we could either be ordered to one of those houses to "back fill" and cover those firehouse areas or called out to the World Trade Center. At this point no one was talking about Al Qaeda or even about how it was a terrorist attack, but when two planes decide to crash into the top floors of two of the most distinct parts of the New York skyline, terrorism is the only explanation that came to mind.

15-20 minutes after I arrived at the firehouse I was reunited with my spare gear and traveling in a pick-up truck with four other firemen out to Rescue 5. From there, we were to join the hundreds of other firefighters from around Staten Island, New Jersey and other places to take a series of buses that would lead us to the ferry that would finally bring us to the island of Manhattan. None of us had any direction yet on what to do once we reached Manhattan, for now we just knew that we needed to get there.

The firefighters were mostly quiet, somber and almost subdued on the series of bus rides. We quietly filed onto the buses and took off to our final destination, the Staten Island Ferry terminal. I didn't really recognize too many guys other than the few that came from the firehouse with me in the pick-up truck. But I did notice that some were choked up, really choked up, silently praying, hoping that the tension would be cut somehow. Usually in the moments before arriving on the scene of a big fire someone will say or do something funny to ease the tension. Guys were usually chomping at the bit, ready to jump into the action and take on the fire or whatever was ahead. Well, not this time. We all knew that serious business was ahead of us. I started to wonder if I had kissed my boys and my wife Judy good-bye for the last time. So, before we reached the Staten Island Ferry, I did something I had never done before.

I was sitting towards the front of the bus but I was facing the back of the bus. This meant that I could see the faces of most of the firefighters who were jammed into the bus with me. I was looking at everyone's individual face. It was quiet. They weren't really talking. There was no muttering, nothing. This was definitely an anomaly. That's when I thought to myself that I needed to pray and I guess these guys needed a little prayer too. I figured that the worst that could happen is someone might give me the kind of look that lets me know they want to call me an altar boy or everything but a child of God, but they'd still listen.

They must have been relieved when I stood up on the bus and broke the silence. I said, "Listen guys, bow your head for a minute. We don't know what we're doing but we need God's help," and I started saying the Lord's Prayer right in front of them as loud as I could and I heard the words resonate throughout the bus as everybody joined in.

I'm not sure what made me get up there and just pray like that, it wasn't something I'd done before. I am a Christian person and I go to church on Sunday and try to do the right thing, but I wouldn't say that I'm a Holy Roller kind of guy. I just knew that we could never be facing a bigger call than this or we'd all be dead already. So I just prayed. By the time we finished praying we were already at the Staten Island Ferry terminal.

Just as we reached the ferry, the towers came crashing down within minutes of each other. I never saw the buildings actually come down, but we were close enough so that I knew what happened. There wasn't anything else that could explain that sound. Even one hundred trains crashing into each other at the same time couldn't make that sound. When we all looked up we saw two columns of cement ash, smoke and papers fluttering in the wind, all outlining the place where the towers once stood. We couldn't see the towers...we couldn't see anything. None of us had radios on us, so there was no communication with the team on the site to get more details. All we had were our own personal equipment, hand tools and gear.

Shortly thereafter the ferry took off towards Manhattan. The ferry glided across New York Bay under a clear blue sky that could only be described as perfect. I knew that the closer we got to Manhattan, the more the iconic Statue of Liberty was supposed to come into focus, but the beautiful clear blue day was interrupted by the ominous rolling fog of dark ash, dust and vapors that radiated from the area where the towers once stood. We couldn't really see well. I paused to wonder how strange it was that just a few hours ago all of us were in completely different places doing many different tasks, chores and jobs were now gathered together in full gear without using or even seeing a fire truck ...and all of a sudden...BOOM! Manhattan... The cavalry has arrived as the ferry slammed me from my thoughts and shook me back to reality and the dock at the very same instant. The ferry collided into the Manhattan terminal with a loud sound that boldly announced that it was time for the boat's anxious and eager passengers to disembark.

As I made my way to the front of the ferry, my mind kept trying to process everything that was going on. There wasn't a single car horn blowing in the city that was known for being in an eternal gridlock. There wasn't a single bird chirping. There wasn't a single person shouting at pedestrians in an attempt to promote their upcoming event political cause or their knock-off Rolex's I affectionately refer to as *Rulex*. In fact there was no sound at all. The usual smell of greasy foods from the roach coach street vendors was replaced with the thick choking smell of fire mixed with smoke and ash. All around me I could feel individual particles of soot and grit flying freely through the air. I knew it was best not to open my mouth to speak unless I needed to. I've experienced the unpleasant taste of ash and grime more than a hundred times before and I did not feel the desire to relive the experience if I didn't need to.

With all the clues I had from the silence that haunted my ears, the singed smell that assaulted my nose and the gritty feel on my neck, hands and any other exposed skin, I still couldn't believe what my eyes were showing me. Depending on the extent of the breeze, I might be able to see four feet ahead of me or twenty feet ahead of me at any given moment. Even during those moments of low visibility, I was able to make out the two to three inches of ash that cloaked the dock and the streets like well-polluted snow. The road of ash captivated me as I took my first steps off the ferry onto the docks-leaving well-defined indelible boot prints behind me.

As I looked up, I noticed the throngs of silent New Yorkers walking solemnly towards the ferry boat so they could escape the horror that I had yet to lay my own eyes on. Each of them was balancing two to three inches of ash on top of their heads.

Manhattan usually draws people with dreams and aspirations for building the next Fortune 500 Company, becoming the greatest Rockette in Radio City Music Hall history or even those who aspire to take the fashion industry by storm. Manhattan is usually full of dreamers, optimists and ambitious souls who are the type to never let set-backs dissuade them and never believe in defeat. But as I watched them walk towards the ferry that I was leaving, I didn't see the stubborn perseverance and hope I was used to. Instead I saw teary eyes that wore blank looks of disbelief or exhibited outright shell shock.

There was no way this was the city of Manhattan that I had known my whole life. I'm a Brooklyn native, but everyone ends up on the island at some point or another. I had even worked at a couple of firehouses out here over the years. This couldn't be real. The city that was usually so vivacious and full of a kaleidoscope of color was now reduced to three colors: light gray, dark gray and black. I thought I was on the set of a black and white movie. Suddenly a woman grabbed my arm, looked into my eyes and said, "God be with you!" No amount of training or experience I had since joining the

FDNY on February 5, 1984 could have ever prepared me for this. I had no idea what to expect next.

As we were walking, we could smell the fires. I got to the corners of Liberty and Church and I knew exactly where I was. I had been there a hundred times before. I was standing right under the street signs. The towers should have been right in front of me, not even a couple hundred feet away to my left. There was so much smoke around me that I couldn't really see or breathe. And most of what I could see was on fire. I was standing still and trying to focus my eyes on what was around me as the wind gently blew an opening in the curtain of smoke that allowed me to quickly view the space where the World Trade Center towers were supposed to be. I stood there stunned...and I didn't understand why I just saw-well, I couldn't believe what I just saw. I look up again to re-read the street signs and they still read the same names I saw before, Liberty and Church Streets. I was stunned because when I looked at what should have been two architectural marvels I saw about 20 stories of steel piled on top of each other. They looked like pick-up sticks.

I looked down at my steel hand tool, a *halligan* that we use to pry open doors and I looked back up at the leveled building, which would soon become known as *The Pile*, and I wondered what we were supposed to be able to accomplish with these tools. When I was in *Proby School* starting my quest to become a firefighter, I learned how to use tools to force doors, create holes, or vent, the roof that would make the fire less likely to create an explosion. We learned to force open doors with steel tools to rescue people trapped in flaming buildings. We learned to safely navigate through large smoky buildings while completely in the dark so that we could help anyone who was trapped inside and find the flames so that the Engine

Company could come in and put out the fire. In my more recent days with the Staten Island firehouse, I learned more about how to wrestle mangled cars to free the passengers trapped inside after horrible accidents. I even learned how to recover people from terrible train accidents. But at that moment, I just didn't understand how any of that experience with those tools would help me take on the wreckage of two 110-story buildings. There was nothing we could do with those tools against all of that steel. So what were we supposed to do?

CHAPTER TWO

Moonlighting Premonition

When my father was a cop with the NYPD, there was no such thing as moonlighting. You couldn't have another job because they figured if you did you were in the mob. You had to be doing something wrong. It was not allowed. You'd get fired from any kind of job. I guess if your family had a business that might have been something else, but for the most part nobody did. There was really no such thing as over time. You just worked when you worked. But this wasn't true for firefighters.

I'm not sure if it was because we were a different type of organization or if it was because we lived in a different time from my father, but nearly every firefighter I ever knew had a part-time job that they went to when they left the firehouse. This was especially true if they had kids. It wasn't uncommon for firemen to work construction or go to school. Mike Wernick was a brilliant guy who attended graduate school to become an architect while he was working in one of the busiest firehouses in the world. He used to stay up all night with pots of coffee in the basement building these little models in preparation for tests. He actually did become a full-fledged architect while he was a firefighter.

One of the best side-gigs I ever picked up was with Hollywood. Kurt, the new chief's aide, asked the members of the 9th battalion if they would like to be in a new movie. He was getting ready to retire and follow his new career as a model/actor and he found a role that was a great transition between the two careers. He needed about 35 off duty firefighters for a few days. Knowing that I would be off for the next few days I quickly volunteered.

We would be paid as the lowest grade non-official stunt men, or as glorified extras. I made the cut and was instructed to report at 6 PM the following evening downtown to the front of 2 Broadway with all of our personal firefighter gear in tow. It was probably less expensive to pay us to bring the real gear than to hire real actors and supply them with gear. Not to mention driving the city's spare fire trucks that the fire department provided. So we reported with some spare city rigs and we become the official firefighters in the 1989 blockbuster movie "Ghostbusters 2."

I had never before seen the inner workings of a Hollywood big budget film, nevertheless been a part of one. I was getting a paid part! $30 an hour was much more than the city was paying me. Not a bad gig. In fact, it was the best side job I ever had. And I have had some shitty ones along the way. Who's complaining? You do whatever someone else doesn't want to do and that's why you got the crappy job in the first place.

Ok, now back to being a star actor... I mean a glorified scrub extra. We were treated very well by all of the staff. We were managed by the *wrangler*, or assistant to the assistant producer's assistant, who had the job of *wrangling* or rounding us up to be ready to hurry up and wait. A head count for now then go help yourself to the large assortment of specially prepared food. There was salad, coffee, candy prepared for the A-listers consisting of Bill Murray, Dan

Aykroyd, Sigourney Weaver, Ernie Hudson, Harold Ramis, Rick Moranis and of course...me.

Still the Johnny-on-the-set in the pecking order of firefighters, I was selected by the senior members to make the all crucial beer runs to the all night deli. Between my hurry up and wait cycles, I was fortunate to meet and talk to Sigourney Weaver who, by the way, is so much more beautiful in person than she appears in the movies. I was even allowed to take photos with her wearing my helmet as well as photos with Bill Murray and Ernie Hudson. They treated me as if I were one of them and were especially interested in my career as one of the city's Bravest.

When they finally decided it was time to shoot my role in the movie they rolled no less than 10 cameras from all different angles and platforms simultaneously with accuracy and professionalism. I was sure they would have captured many of us in one particular scene when all the stars were present and acting in their rolls. I guess a lot of the great footage that was shot while I was front and center ended up on the cutting room floor because I definitely wasn't in the final film for long. My film debut was not as exemplary as I had planned. My Hollywood career was brief. Although if you happen to view it on a DVD or late night TV, one hour twenty six minutes and seventeen seconds into the film is proof that I earned my pay. There is a head shot of two firefighters looking up. I'm the firefighter on the right. Ta Da! I exit stage left.

During my 20 years as a firefighter I often worked construction on my off-duty days and left behind any aspirations of becoming a full-time actor. But I spent many of my later years driving limos.

One of the easiest limo driving nights I've ever had was also one of the scariest. On July 4, 2000 I was hired out to drive an older couple out to dinner to celebrate their anniversary and the nation's birthday. The part that made the job so easy was that it was only a 4.5 mile drive from where they lived to their destination. When I picked them up I met a really nice guy who just got a promotion and was excited about celebrating his big day, his anniversary and the nation's birthday in style with his lady. That is why he chose to take her to dinner at the Windows of the World restaurant atop the beautiful World Trade Center. At 9 pm multiple barges would take their positions in the Hudson River and unleash an amazing fireworks display that would be watched on televisions around the country. But for this couple, they would see it through the large open windows of the iconic World Trade Center.

When I drive, I would usually open the door and let the guests into the car, drive them to their destination and then open the door to let them out. I'd wait around somewhere until they were ready to leave and then repeated the same process to take them home. But this time the gentleman invited me to have dinner, on him, at the bar in the restaurant. No one had ever offered me such a generous tip. Since it was my nation that was celebrating a birthday too I thought I should take a minute to celebrate like everyone else. So I let them go upstairs first while I looked for a parking spot.

Finding a parking spot in Manhattan near the World Trade Center on the 4th of July is about as simple as performing heart surgery with only a bottle of rubbing alcohol and a plastic butter knife, so when I found a spot only a block away that could hold the limo I knew it was my lucky night. Because there were locals and tourists all over the city looking for a place to camp out before the fireworks started, there were cops everywhere. I notice an officer standing on the corner near the spot I hoped to claim as my own. The space wasn't near a fire hydrant but I thought it best to ask before I risked having my work vehicle towed before my gig was over. So I approached the officer.

"Hi. My name is Ron Parker and I'm a firefighter, my dad was a police officer. He told me that if I ever needed a favor to just ask. Will you be here all night?"

"Yes, I'll be here until the fireworks are over."

"Is it alright if I leave my limo here?"

"Sure, you're fine."

"Thanks! I appreciate it!"

I locked up the vehicle and went upstairs to claim a good spot at the bar where I could enjoy my free meal and watch the fireworks. It would have been nice to have my wife and my boys with me, but the food and the view was great and served as a decent consolation prize.

Now I've never been one to believe in visions, premonitions or séance's or anything of the sort, but while I was looking out of the window a sense of panic overtook me. My palms and my forehead started to sweat, my tuxedo started to feel like it was getting tight and choking me and every bit of my senses were screaming at me to get out of this place. The restaurant was filled with the normal chatter and clanging of silverware on plates that were being relieved of their food, but there was nothing out of place going on. It didn't matter, because everything in me was telling me to get out of here before the building fell. As a firefighter who, at this time, already had over 15 years of experience running into the very situations that everyone else was trying to get out of, panic of this level was foreign to me. So I did the only thing I could do, I called the server and reminded him of the table that was covering my bill, left a tip and ran back to the limo.

I must have startled the officer because he looked surprised to see me as I quickly unlocked the driver's side door.

"We still have time before the fireworks start. You don't have to leave just now. You're fine."

"Thanks, but I gotta go."

I quickly maneuvered the limo out of its spot and drove several blocks north, away from the World Trade Center where I stayed on Chambers and West St. until I got the call from my passengers telling me that they were ready to leave.

I didn't tell the passengers about why I left so quickly. I didn't tell my wife about that moment. But as I stood on the corner of Liberty and Church looking for the building that housed the restaurant where I had that panic attack, I was in awe.

I didn't stay there long because a chief suddenly appeared. With wide, bloodshot and teary eyes he welcomed and thanked us for the quick response and directed us towards Broadway. These orders puzzled us because Broadway was not the most direct path to *The Pile*. I guessed that maybe they wanted to break us down into teams and give us specific tasks. This normally wasn't necessary because every fireman in the firehouse has an assigned role to play. We find out what our role is as soon as we report for duty. But there was nothing normal about this situation. Instead of having two or three firehouses report to a scene, this was an all-city all-borough call of every firefighter, on duty and off duty, and with thousands of first responders anxious to serve and so we needed a plan and a strategy quick. All of us were out on Broadway in front of City Hall while the chiefs worked together to build a new command center that would bring order to the situation.

I found out later that my guess was only partially correct. While there were a couple hundred firefighters standing with me out on Broadway there was a desperate rescue taking place at the time. We only knew that we had a direct order from a battalion chief that we needed to listen to. Without question, they didn't want hundreds of firemen clambering around because they had limited, if not lost, radio communications with trapped and lost firefighters with rescued survivors in the stairwell of the North Tower.

One of those trapped firefighters was a friend of mine, Lieutenant Mickey Kross. He was there with 13 other people-11 firefighters, a port authority police officer and a civilian secretary named Josephine. They were all trapped between the third and the fifth floors after the North Tower collapsed. Outside the tower, all efforts were desperately being made to find these trapped and injured survivors with the faint and limited radio communication. Inside the North tower, the crew didn't know that the whole North Tower had just completely collapsed.

The History Channel documentary "The Miracle of Stairway B" describes how the trapped firefighter rescue crew would try to direct the firefighters outside to their location.

"Well, yeah. We're in the North Tower."

And the firefighter responds to them, "Where's the North Tower?"

"What do you mean 'where's the North Tower'? We're in stairwell B in the North Tower-copy stairwell B."

The building that was erect just minutes before was now gone. It was a cruel magic trick that produced a daunting task for the exhausted chiefs- many of whom had just miraculously escaped the tower's quick deadly tumble with their own lives.

Although I'm sure that none of us would blame the chiefs for not taking a moment to sit down with us and talk us through all the horrific details of what our brothers were experiencing in stairway B of the North Tower, we were quickly becoming bored and anxious with waiting. Don't get me wrong, there was activity, but those of us who weren't a part of it yet were the anxious ones. There were teams putting out raging fires and pushing hose lines forward to the Trade Center while the lieutenants were trying to work with the firefighters and captains to deploy strategic rescue teams and get them on their way as quickly and efficiently as humanly possible.

The chiefs were holding us back because they didn't want any of their men to get into more trouble than they could handle at the time. The buildings were on fire, the cars were on fire and the streets were on fire, so the chiefs had all the primary streets blocked and they were handpicking guys to go down with hose lines to put out the vehicle fires. They were trying to make a path down more selected streets for us to move into the crushed and flaming towers of death and debris. Until they had a way to know where everyone was going and a strategy for keeping us safe while we rescue the civilians, we were to stay put.

While the chiefs worked diligently to get communications up and running for a command center, there were men like my friend Jimmy Falcone who served as interim messengers. When the chiefs heard that there was someone with a bicycle that could maneuver around the 25 acres of ruins, he was quickly recruited as a messenger. However, that wasn't why he was there.

I played many a great hockey game as well as a good softball game with my friend, Jimmy Falcone. He is a brother firefighter who I worked with on a lot of tours out on Avenue U in Brooklyn. Jimmy worked as hard as a Mason pouring concrete. He always gave 100% for his fellow firefighters, his family and his friends. But he also gave his all to a family tradition handed down from his grandfather, to his dad and then to him. He also had a passion for sports.

I called him the Pied Piper because he had a wonderful way of inventing and creating new and fun ways that kids could perform hockey drills without being bored. He ran the local recreation center's roller hockey league. He was a certified referee and instructor who was well schooled in the rules. He always managed to even out the sides or the score by calling the well placed penalty shot as time withered off the clock while he secretly hoped the game would be brought to overtime. It wasn't ever about winning or losing. He loved to teach the kids regardless of their ability and they all knew it and loved him for it. In a short time he could take kids that no one wanted on the team and he would evaluate their talents, help them strengthen their skills and coach them all while having fun in transforming them into team superstars. Jim did this easily. All the parents loved his total dedication to seeing that the kids had a great time. He would even make the rounds to pick up the kids from their home if they didn't have a ride. This was all volunteer work, but that was the kind of Pied Piper guy he was.

Jimmy was working that day as a member of Ladder 153. As the terrible moments unfolded, Jimmy needed to get to the Trade Center quickly. His sister was working downtown that day within earshot of the World Trade Center and he couldn't get in touch with her because all of the phone lines were jammed. One of the brothers was working on his vehicle in front of the quarters that morning and Jimmy quickly assigned him his riding position on Ladder 153. He quickly notified an officer, grabbed his gear and left the quarters of Engine 254, Ladder 153 and proceeded to the car service on the corner of Avenue U and Coney Island Avenue. His demands for a ride to the World Trade Center were initially met with protest, but the driver finally agreed and started the 10 mile drive to the Trade Center.

He should have arrived within in minutes, but the NYPD halted all traffic heading in that direction and exclusively reserved passage through the Prospect Expressway to emergency vehicles. Grateful for the gear he had with him, Jimmy immediately fled the taxi and hitchhiked a ride into the city in one of the NYPD cruisers. By the time his chauffeured squad car reached the foot of the Brooklyn Bridge his journey was stopped again. This time the delay was caused by a report that bridges and tunnels into the city were being targeted for bombing by terrorists. With this news, Jimmy quickly suggested that the officer driving the vehicle re-route to the Brooklyn Battery Tunnel which was only a mile or so away.

When they arrived they found an Engine blocking the entrance. No one was being allowed through the tunnel either. Jimmy saddled up next to the chauffeur in the Engine and learned that the rest of the Engine Company was dispersed throughout the tunnel for radio relay with the towers. After their brief conversation, the chauffeur looked away for a moment and Jimmy suddenly started running towards the mouth of the tunnel. Running downhill wasn't so bad as he passed the bewildered relay radio Engine men halfway through the tunnel, but when he started the upward climb on the other side of the tunnel that opened up to Manhattan, he had to remind himself that he was pushing through the pain to rescue his sister.

In no time he saw a small jeep-like personal vehicle approaching him from the other direction. The driver was Mattie James, the Uniformed Firefighter Association's Brooklyn delegate and the passenger was the captain of the Engine Company who had just deployed his men throughout the tunnel in hope of successfully completing the necessary relay of information from Brooklyn to Manhattan. They instructed him to get in the jeep so they could carry him back to the Brooklyn side of the tunnel, but he took off again in a flash like a deranged bumble bee on a mission. As he exited the tunnel on the Manhattan side he found an abandoned bicycle and a small shovel that he taped under the frame of the bike and proceeded to Ground Zero-now fully mobile.

I caught up with Jimmy late that morning before we would be deployed on Broadway. He had received word that his sister was safely out of Manhattan. By this time he was the official communications liaison of Ground Zero. He endlessly peddled the bike all around the destruction to relay and dispatch orders between the chiefs. I told Jimmy that he looked like he was in the French Underground as he was now only wearing his fireman's helmet, shorts, gloves and boots to make his appointed rounds.

Just about that time I looked up as I heard a familiar roar of an engine. It was not just any engine, but the roar of a Harley Davidson motorcycle making its way through the dense smoke and haze towards us. Pulling right up before me and Jimmy was Tim Duffy, another member of the "Watchdawgs," the nickname for Brooklyn Ladder 153.

This is not at all what usually happens on a call. It's a well-orchestrated dance and you'd better know what you're doing. Each firehouse is typically the home of one Engine Company and one Truck Company. The Truck Company is also referred to as a Ladder Company. The Engine Company is the five-person team who operates the hose and puts the fire out, and the Truck Company is the six-person team that goes into the building first to perform forcible entry, rescues, locate the flames and vent the building to prevent an explosion or any additional damage from pent up super heat and flames that can't escape.

When the Engine arrives on the scene, it has to find the closest hydrant to the building without passing it and then prepare to go in by hooking up to the hydrant and stretching the line.

Once the Truck Company arrives, they force their way into a building that does not want to help them put that fire out. The chauffeur stays with the truck and operates the ladder if needed. Often they may position the ladder to help the *roof man* reach the roof so he can tear a hole in it to provide a place for the smoke, flames and steam to flood through as it tries to hide from the Engine Company as they attack it with the water. Otherwise the steam, smoke and flames may blow back into the faces of the Engine Company. The Truck team also has an *OV* person, or *outside vent.* This is the person who opens or breaks the back windows to provide additional vents for the fire. Although the *roof man* and *OV* are solo positions that are usually assigned to the most experienced firemen in the truck, the officer and the other two men on the truck go in as a team-*the forcible entry team.*

The forcible entry team is the *can man,* usually the junior guy because the position allows him to stay with the officer, who has a fire extinguisher and a *hook*. The other person on this team is the *irons man*. Here's the guy that has the break-in tools. He's got the axe and the *halligan*, which is that pry bar that can break anything. I've never seen one break. I've never seen one bend. I've seen it run over by a train, but never broken. He also has the *k-tool* or the *rabbit tool* that can force the doors pneumatically.

The primary objective of the forcible entry team is to force entry as quickly, efficiently and safely as possible. Even under duress and extreme dangerous deadly conditions because every precious second counts. Many times the team faces an endless array of cleverly placed unconventional locking systems. In a multi-cultural state like New York, it was not uncommon to come across new European or Asian locks, brought in and professionally installed by immigrants, that would impede our necessary entry to the premises. And just when you think you got it you discover that there's another lock backing up the one you just took off.

Military C-4 explosives were not included in the repertoire of the New York City's fire departments use and training, although I'm sure some chiefs would like to have included the explosive material with the rest of the equipment of the rescue and squad companies. However, we've come across some doors and locks that would've rendered even the use of explosives unsuccessful. Some drug dealers have even devised illegal traps and incendiary deterrents of their own such as cleverly hidden balloons filled with gasoline to greet us upon entering their lair. Many of their homemade devices for keeping the unwanted out could should probably be adopted for use on 46th Street's Jewelers Diamond Way-also known as the diamond district.

We trained very often and for long periods of time in the firehouse as well as on *The Rock*-the 11 building Bureau of Training site on Randall's Island-on the very serious subject of forcible entry. We are trained and retrained as smooth cat burglars who can bypass intricate locking systems without always using brute force. We size up the severity of the situation on how to approach our task and many times very little damage is done to the existing door because we only attack the locking system. Urgency and time is a large part of the determination. Some of the master tools we use have been invented by career criminals whose specialty is the art of burglary. These self-trained devious thieves are highly skilled and very intelligent. I sometimes wondered what would have happened if these criminals would have used their knowledge to serve mankind, instead of stealing from mankind. If they would've legally patented these devices for the fire, police and military as well as locksmiths, they may have been financially rewarded greatly, possibly deterring them from a life of crime.

A career thief was caught with burglary tools that included a *k-tool* device and the arresting officers didn't even know what it was or how to use it. The arrested tool's inventor asked for leniency and in exchange he would explain what it was and how it was used to bypass many of our city's inhabitants safely guarded doors very quietly and quickly. This tool is now a main staple used very effectively by every Truck Company in the city of New York.

There's a whole lot of action going on real fast. I remember a saying that says "it's countless hours of mundane placid days, interrupted by seconds of sheer terror." As I stood on Broadway remembering the glimpse of *The Pile* I saw only minutes before, I knew that there were more than a few seconds of sheer terror ahead of me.

I'll admit that I was probably more impatient than most. I was pacing like a caged tiger although I knew it was a waste of energy. At the time I didn't know what was going on and I was ready to move. So I took it upon myself to cut through adjacent buildings so I could go see what was going on down at the World Trade Center. My dad and I used to run a small soda business on Wall Street for brokerage houses. So I learned how to cut through buildings and how to use the back alleys so that I always had a place to park our old beat up van, out of the sight of police, when I delivered the sodas using the freight elevators at the back of the buildings. Sometimes I would snake in between buildings to get more deliveries in. Now that all of us were in a holding pattern and didn't know what was going on, I decided this was a good time to make good use of my old skills. Besides, the police were already upset with all the firefighters collecting in one spot and making it impassable, so I gave them a little more room by leaving.

I knew I couldn't take anybody with me because I didn't even know where I was going and I didn't want to create a stir. So I acted like I needed to go to the bathroom and I snaked my way through maybe three or four buildings. There were a lot of dead ends. It took a little bit of doing but at the same time, that was good because these guys were putting fires out in the vehicles that were burning, so by the time I got out on the street a lot of those vehicle fires were out and I could make it past without anybody seeing me. I came out near the US Post Office on the northeast corner of the World Trade Center. I was butted up against the building and cautiously sliding across because glass, metal and concrete were falling all over the place. I couldn't really see that well, obviously, but you could hear stuff falling and you could see flames reaching out of the building.

I was able to make it to the corner of the postal building and when I turned and I saw an Engine that was hooked up and pumping across from a World Trade Center tower. That's when I saw maybe thirteen, fourteen, or fifteen floors all on fire from almost three or four windows in. Almost the whole side of the building was on fire. I also realized that I wasn't going to be able to make it inside the building to help because flames were literally everywhere and glass and debris and all kinds of stuff that I couldn't recognize were flying in every direction.

In *Proby School*, we have something we called a "confidence course" where they blindfold you with your full gear on, blacked out your mask and told you, "Here's the door. Walk through it and get to the other side. We'll be waiting for you. "You were a mouse in a maze that the instructors created for you. They had all kinds of traps waiting for you. There were guys that would put hooks on the back of your masks, like you were caught on something. You didn't know what it was that hooked onto your gear. You had to stop and figure out which way to roll around and unhook yourself from the bicycle or whatever was stopping you. They had locked doors that you had to open. There were missing floors and you had to know how to walk across a beam to get across. You had to feel which way the beams were going. You had to squeeze through all kinds of stuff and now you're squeezing through a partially collapsed building. They had everything there. You had to do it before you ran out of air. Let me tell you, you had to do it correctly the first time. You didn't have time for error because if you took a long time you were finished.

You had to pace your breathing because you didn't know how much more you had to climb through. Only the instructors have ever seen the entire course from beginning to end with the benefit of full daylight. And it didn't matter if you had a buddy who had been through it before and tried to give you tips because the instructors often moved the doors, walls, windows and everything else in the maze. The instructors were watching you and each move you made was silently being rated. As ingenious as the invention was when I was in *Proby School*, there were no simulations like what I saw before me on my way to the towers. I can't even imagine how they would simulate something like this.

A friend of mine used to own a bar right across the street from the World Trade Center. At the time he was calling it "New York, New York." I used to go there after work. So did dozens of people who worked in the World Trade Center or other places in the area. That bar was always packed. There would be crowds looking for dinner, drinks and dancing every Friday night and big stakes card games in the basement on the weekends. It really was a great place. There was always something going on in the city and that was one of the places where things usually happened, but not now. The only things happening at this time were fires, flying ash, falling debris and first responders looking for civilians and other first responders who may have been trapped in the collapsed buildings. All the people who made Manhattan come to life were riding out of the city as fast as they could on ferry boats and anything else that would get them out of there.

CHAPTER THREE

Bowels of Hell

I cut across the street and saw the Engines pumping water. They were hooked up to the hydrants, so I tried to figure out what Engine Company was there and looked underneath the truck to see if there was anyone nearby.

"Anybody? Anybody? Fireman? Fireman!" I yelled. Nobody answered.

Then I ran across the street making quick and deliberate movements. I dodged falling debris and crawled over unidentifiable smoldering heaps. I never saw a single person as I made my way across what was usually one of the busiest streets in the city. There was usually gridlock, but now I couldn't find a single person. Once I made it to the opposite side of the street, I was right next to what was left of the North Tower. All of the cars on the curb were on fire, so I looked into the car windows to see if maybe somebody survived.

"Anybody? Anybody? Anybody here? Anybody..."

I just kept hearing myself say that over and over as I made my way down the street toward the North Tower and stopping every five steps to peer into the cars near me. I did not find a single survivor in any of those vehicles.

So I went back to the Engine and saw that the suction hose was connected to the hydrant and was actively pumping water through the hose. This told me that there should be firemen holding the other end of the hose and attacking the flames. This meant that all I needed to do was follow the hose to find them. But I couldn't make it into the building. I tried many different times from different angles, but instead of doorways and hallways there were 75 foot deep stories of steel lying on top of each other like pancakes. There was barely enough space to look in between the layers of steel, let alone crawl between them to enter the remains of what used to be buildings. It was simply impassible. I couldn't even see where the hose line had gone, or the firemen who had hooked it up.

The building foundation is 7-8 stories deep and the home of the Port Authority of NY & NJ, or PATH as we called it, operated a train service beneath the World Trade Center that connected about 250,000 people on its Newark-World Trade Center and Hoboken-World Trade Center routes as well as to the New York City Subway trains that also picked up passengers at the station. PATH was connected to the building by a concourse and a shopping center that was simply known as "The Mall at the World Trade Center." So at ground level you could go 7-8 stories under.

I was a member of Truck Companies for most of my career, so I was in search and rescue mode. I put my helmet on the debris and figured that if I got trapped in there, somebody would see the helmet and it would work as a distress signal. For a firefighter, you throw your helmet out the window and they know that someone's missing and what company you're from. I was trying to map out where I was and what I saw so when I went back with the other firemen I could tell them whether there was anyone or anything in that space that they needed to go back to. If not, it would be a better use of their time and energy to go to other unexplored areas. They are always welcomed to do a secondary search, but at least they know that the primary has already been complete. At this point, I wasn't even sure if anyone knew I was gone yet. Besides, the whole reason they had us waiting was because they had too many guys at the moment without specific assignments.

I crawled into the underground mall. Once I was inside I saw that the ceiling actually met the floor. There was no space between them. The opening just stopped 100 feet in. I couldn't get past anything. I couldn't find anything that was discernible other than the steel beams that were supposed to be holding up the building. After a while I didn't know where up or down was. I had to crawl over something to go down into something. All I could do was look for voids of space where I could crawl deeper into the maze and look for someone. Someone was going to be behind the beam, or somebody was going to be...somewhere waiting for help. That's why I had to get there.

I wasn't worried about getting stuck in a dead end or running into any trouble in the buildings. I was on a mission to be there for whoever needed help. If anyone asked what I was doing, I was ready to tell them I was looking for a restroom, but I knew that waiting around was not for me. I needed to get there. I needed to get the job done.

Everything was on fire. Every time I looked around I couldn't breathe. I couldn't see. I was crawling on stuff. I tried to crawl in further but I just reached a dead end. I could hear the military jets high above and I could hear the firefighter P.A.S.S. alarms going off, but I still couldn't go any further inside. So I turned around and I went back outside. There was nothing there. I didn't find anyone.

I knew that I had been off on my own for too long and that it was time to get back to the muster station and rejoin the firefighters waiting for their orders. As I tracked my way back to the muster station I took several pictures with the cheap disposable camera some firefighters keep with their gear. I knew that no one would believe what I saw, so I had to snap pictures. I wasn't concerned with taking pictures on the way in, but I made sure that I took several on the way out.

It's not like I could walk back like you normally walk down a street. I had to stop and duck and look at what was in front of me. I had to make strategies for getting over, under or around the blazing cars and falling debris. I had to do all this with the snippets of vision I could steal in the midst of all the smoke and ash. The whole time I was out there I wasn't thinking about being afraid. I was too scared to be afraid because you never know what's going to happen. Collapses are similar to earthquakes. When something shifts, who knows what else is going to happen. There's a building next door and it might fall on top of the one you are in. But who knows for sure?

I got past the debris and joined back up with the other firefighters at the muster station on Broadway about 30 minutes after the time I originally left. It looked like the chiefs were making progress with creating teams and sending them out. Finally, we get a group and get assigned to some lieutenant I never heard of. Each team had their own space to cover. Ours was down Trinity Place right past the church near the North Tower. I recognized Billy O'Connor, a 20 year vet from my new firehouse, and we quickly partnered up on the walk down to our group's assigned location. Although I had already been there once on my own, I made sure to take a lot more photos to document everything and study it later. Besides, there was so much going on that I was seeing things on this second walk down there that I had missed the first time-like the cadaver dogs.

Shortly after the attacks there were cadaver dogs out on *The Pile*. They were so confused because the smell of smoke and death was all around them instead of being in concentrated areas. They walked in circles trying to pinpoint individual people in distress or already deceased. Their handlers would not release them and stayed close by with the aid of a leash. I imagined that they were concerned about losing the dogs in one of the many crevices that the canines would squeeze into while they were following different scents. As they walked around it wasn't unusual to hear yelps of pain and see them quickly lick their paws after they were cut open with the exposed pieces of glass or sharp edged steel. I couldn't watch. It was killing me.

Once we reached our assigned area we used a rope to tie ourselves together by the waist. This was called a *search line*. It helped us stay together although we couldn't see each other. It's easy to get disoriented and not know how to get back out if you are on your own, but when you're tied to other firefighters and moving in a line it's easier to account for everybody and simply back up to get out. When we went into the buildings we knew that people were in there because we could hear clambering, but I couldn't see much. Usually when we go in and out of buildings we have our own Scott air masks. But we didn't have any of that this time, our supplies were limited. So we were just hoping to like take a sip of air here and there and hope that things don't go south real fast before you could get out of there.

It was hard to see and hard to breathe inside the buildings. It took 20 minutes to go 20 feet because the wreckage was nearly impassible. We would go up over smoldering office furniture and under fallen beams to make our way through the building. But it seemed like no matter what we did, we would eventually get caught in a dead end somewhere. It was a much tighter squeeze than either of us imagined. We're both pretty big boys and in good shape, but everything was just very tight.

I heard a rescuer scream that he had found somebody. There was somebody yelling, so we definitely had to go further down, up, around the debris to follow the voice. We all quietly stopped and listened. Visibility was sometimes limited to your hand in front of your face. Somewhere there was a firefighter barking for a Stokes basket ahead of us. The message was telephoned person to person until one was located and passed man to man. We pushed, pulled and slithered the Stokes basket over the debris towards the person needing help. The rescuers closer to the civilian reached down through the shards of glass, the steel rods and the unyielding concrete to free the prisoner trapped underneath. Finally successful, they lifted the person up into the basket and secured them in so that the backboard and cervical collar would immobilize them and reduce the risk of further injury before they reach the medical team that was standing by. I don't know who it was, but I know the person was alive. I never saw the person we helped because there were 2 or 3 people in front of me. I was just grateful that we were able to get the person out to safety alive.

Every couple of hours we were able to go outside and get some oxygen and water. Of course we didn't have a lot of liquid in there...so when you go out you wash your eyes out, you get some oxygen and you go back in. You repeat that a couple of times and you keep going down into the piles of danger and debris.

Manhattan has all of these little bodegas everywhere and that's where we would go when we needed some food or water to keep us going. You had to do that to survive and you could only get goods that were sealed. Some guys would take those little power bars but that was about it. It wasn't like we were shopping. We may grab a flashlight or batteries or something else that would help, but it wasn't like we were pillaging. We were procuring anything that might be needed in self-survival knowing we were there for the long haul. Still not knowing if the attack had subsided or, for that matter, what else was going on in the outside world.

I don't remember what time it was, but I remember a woman sitting up on the steps in front of Brooks Brothers, which is a fancy men's clothing store with $5,000 plus suits. The young woman might have been wearing scrubs and she was sitting in a lotus position with her lands out, facing the towers. She didn't say anything as I walked past her and she was as motionless as a mannequin. I didn't know who she was, why she was there or what she was doing. But whatever she was doing actually had a calming effect on me. She seemed to be the only person there who seemed to know what she was doing.

After I passed her I went back in and I kept hearing military jets flying right over our heads. Like supersonic! Zoom! Zoom! Zoom! Not knowing, hearing bits and pieces of other attacks...Washington, DC, Pennsylvania, not knowing if the White House was hit. We didn't know if there were more planes coming in to New York. We were hearing all kinds of stuff, but nobody had any *real* information. We kept getting bits and pieces, but we weren't even thinking about that because we were thinking about what we had to be doing because everybody else had to be doing what they needed to be doing. The military was doing what they had to do and we had no idea what was going on outside. I just knew that we had to keep searching for survivors who desperately needed our help. Time is of the essence and it was running out.

We knew...the first one could be an accident...the second one is not an accident. We didn't know it was Al Qaeda. We suspected it was...because back in February of 1993 they planted a truck bomb in the lower part of the tower. They parked it next to the support column hoping that one building would collapse into the other building...but because of the superior US construction crew that built it fortified the building in such a way that made their plan ineffective. So we knew it was them...who else would it be?

Manhattan is the kind of place where you never went to the same fire twice, not in 20 years. It's not like Brooklyn where you have row after row of frame houses or single occupant dwellings or the projects. Everybody in the Brooklyn firehouses knows that there's the A line, the B line, the C line, the D line to all the same apartments. You can get used to that. In those high-rises you usually spend a lot of time lugging your gear and tools up stairs because the elevator is usually out. By the time you get there you start getting to work. You start forcing doors, you've got to get in, crawl around and your Spiderman's tingly sense is going off all over the place. You're praying that somebody finds this fire. It's getting hot. It's getting dark and your tank is running low on air. That was what I was used to. And what I was crawling through on September 11, 2001 was absolutely nothing like what I was used to.

Most of us had arrived at *The Pile* between 9:30 and 11 am, depending on where we were and whether or not we were on duty when we heard about the towers. The firemen who were on-duty when the first plane hit the north tower were the ones who arrived first. For those of us who had more personal things on our list for the day, like pressure washing the house, it took us a bit longer to arrive. But all of us were there together working our way through *The Piles* of debris putting all of our senses to work in search of people held prisoner in the concrete.

Even late into the afternoon, the sun still shone from its throne in the sky to pierce the still lingering clouds of ash with its rays of light. The warm fall weather that was so inviting just this morning was in stark contrast with the day's events. The peaceful calm and silence that now marked the day seemed to mock us as we clambered across the fiery landscape. As dismal as the day was for me, I couldn't imagine what it must have been like for the people who were at work fiddling with their computer or going from one office to another when they were quickly enveloped in a slide of concrete.

Regardless of how my throat burned from the ash and smoke I inhaled or how my hands bled from scraping against the angry broken glass or how much I sweat and became weary from the constant bending and stooping and crawling and digging, I knew I had to keep going. When I got tired I remembered the cries I had heard from the first person I helped free from the concrete prison. I didn't want someone else's concrete prison to become their grave, so I had to keep moving.

There were times when I would stand still and try to steady my breathing as I slowly and methodically scanned my surroundings for any subtle movements. It wasn't unusual for someone who is trapped to start wiggling a nearby object in hopes of catching someone's attention. I was also listening intently for any cries for help. I was listening for the sounds of shifting metal or concrete in an area where no one was walking. Or worse, I was listening for a cry for help underneath the very concrete where I was standing.

It was a constant struggle to balance my determination to hurry up and help people with the knowledge that a hasty movement could cause me to overlook the slightest sign of distress or even cause me to make someone's situation worse by shifting the debris and closing up the pocket of air they were using to sustain them. How do you act when you know that both your action and/or your inaction may be the difference between someone living or dying? This is a question that I had always considered early on in my career, but it was never as relevant as it was now.

Around 5:30 pm, all of the rescuers were given the order to stay where we were and not to move. At the time, I was about 300 feet away from 7 World Trade Center in a ring of burning buildings. I had all but blocked the fires out of my focus because I was so honed in on the search and rescue. But moments after I received the order to stop moving, 7 World Trade Center, a 52 plus story flame assaulted building across the street from the Towers that was just beside where I was standing, lost its battle with the wind and gravity and crumbled to the ground and sent a fresh crop of cement, steel, glass, dust, ash as well as spilling its tons of contents through the air along with a trail of smoke. As I watched it crumble I held on to the closest North Tower girder in hopes that it would support me and help me avoid being sucked under the newly created pile. All the dust that was already there on the ground was kicked up all over again. With the imminent threat now over, my brother firemen and I continued combing through the piles in search of our fellow New Yorkers in the few hours of daylight we had left.

It was around this time that my heroes arrived-the iron and steel workers. These guys were carrying acetylene torches down the street and trying to make their way with what looked like small cranes. I don't know where they got the equipment from but they just came out of nowhere and stayed with us. A common propane flame burns at 3,630 degrees Fahrenheit, but the acetylene torches they were carrying could burn at about 6,330 degrees Fahrenheit. These torches could slice through many types of metal with ease and could quickly weld pieces together to make any kind of make-shift recovery tools that we could imagine. These made-on-the-spot tools were much more effective than any gear that firefighters typically carry.

They'd say, "What do you need? What do you want us to cut?" They didn't give up. They were there. They made the tools that we were missing. They were the ones that made an impact. Their eagerness to jump in there with us and help gave me an extra boost that helped me get through the night. These rugged hard core men saddled up and dug in. They took a terrible feed from the horrible smoke and ash permeating their lungs but they never complained. They steadily worked while sweating, bleeding and exerting all the energy that a person could possibly expend. These unsung heroes are the back bone of laborers who have made America great. I will never look at any of our nation's construction workforce the same after their sacrifice I witnessed in the bowels of hell.

As the evening rolled in, more information was available about which personnel were confirmed to be at work and which were still being reported as missing. There were two Port Authority police officers trapped in the South Tower. For possibly the hundredth time that day, we stood shoulder-to-shoulder to form a human chain that traveled through, up, down and all around the debris. There were actually two chains that were facing each other so that we could safely and quickly pass the two Stokes baskets carrying the injured officers through our hands to the medics. These were two more people we were able to get out of the wreckage alive. They were the very last people to escape the grasp of the mangled fiery tomb with their lives.

After the men were moved to safety, Billy O'Connor, who had been working beside me most of the day, continued climbing through *The Pile* looking for signs of life. This time we came across a dusty gray hose line. We instinctively followed the line to the nozzle and started aiming at the fire that was all around us. Within seconds we shifted from being Ladder guys who do search and rescue to Engine guys taking on the flames. Every firefighter is trained to do everything, so it was not unusual for us to switch tasks as necessary. At this time of night, it was already hard to see-even with the large work lights from the construction crews. So we thought that we might as well make use of the hose we found to stop the flames from sucking up any oxygen that anyone buried beneath the rubble may need to survive until we got to them.

Although switching from Ladder work to Engine work was not unusual, it was very unusual to find an unattended hose lying around. No firefighter ever leaves their tools, equipment or hose line under any circumstances. If a fireman was having trouble breathing and could no longer handle the hose line, he would rather die holding the hose line than pass it to someone in another company. That's just our culture. We do what needs to be done at any and all cost. So the fact that we found the line lying there meant that the men who pulled it off the truck and hooked it up to the hydrant were most likely buried under the carnage like the hose we had unearthed. We didn't see any signs of life while we were there, so I could only hope that the men who had worked that line before were already carried away to a hospital.

It seemed like no matter how much water we forced onto the flames, they would not go out. We pushed on and kept trying, but around 1:30 in the morning Billy and I agreed that we had done all that our bodies would allow us to do. We had been at *The Pile* for over 12 hours doing search and rescue and fighting flames. We were shot. We were finished. We could no longer hold the hose. We could no longer force our minds or our bodies to do anything.

We turned to crawl back out through the maze we had entered. It took us about 20-30 minutes to maneuver through the dark and follow the hose line back out to the Engine it was connected to. The hose line snaked up and down and round and round. We knew that we were going the right way because we were following the "bumps to the pumps."

When firemen are going into a building, they have 50 feet sections of hose they can connect to each other to adjust the hose line length to reach the flames. At the end of the hoses, where they are connected to each other, is where the braille like bump is located. When you put two hoses together, one has the bump and one doesn't. The bump to the right, or the bump out, is "bumps to the pumps," and the pump is outside in the Engine. So if you follow bumps to the pumps you're going to get out, you're not going to go the wrong way. So, we went up, down, all around, following the hose out. It's not a direct line and with us being so mentally and physically drained, it felt like it was taking forever.

Once we made it back out onto the street, Billy and I went back to 110 Liberty Street to the new triage center so we could get more water and oxygen. As soon as we get a doctor's attention so that we can get our oxygen, the doctor makes an announcement.

"Ok, three strikes, you're out."

"Wait a minute," I asked puzzled, "what are you talking about?"

"You've been here three times."

We hadn't noticed that each time we came to triage to get water and oxygen the staff would mark our coats with a grease pencil. Our coats already had two marks on them, so now that we were back a third time they were going to ship us out to a full hospital in an ambulance. It was another policy that came down from the chiefs to make sure that we all stayed safe. It made sense, but we still didn't like it. We were tired and just ready to go home, but we knew there was no use trying to fight the protocol, so we rode off in the ambulance.

What we saw at the hospital was almost as somber as what we had just left at *The Pile*. No less than 30 unused, clean and empty gurneys in neat rows greeted us at the entrance of the hospital. There was no one lying in them. There were no doctors or nurses. Just empty gurney's waiting to be filled with the same people we had been carrying out of the wreckage in Stokes baskets. It was already disheartening to see so many monumental structures crumble before our eyes back at ground zero, but now that we were at the hospital we were faced with the consequences that those compromised buildings placed on the people who once occupied them. This was almost too much.

We went inside and the team on duty gave us oxygen and checked our lungs and everything else on us to make sure we were okay. We were both tired and had a few bruises from crawling around the concrete jungle gym, but we were okay.

When we saw a chief come in with a heart attack we exchanged wide eyed looks that made it clear that we were thinking the same thing-we had to get out of there. We knew that everything we experienced that day was the kind of thing that you couldn't forget. But watching a chief who was out there with us on *The Pile* struggle for his life was simply too much. Decades on the job had trained us to be tough guys who have the strength to take on the challenges that most people run from. But with 14 hours and counting of being physically and mentally challenged followed by the emotional pain of seeing one more member of the brotherhood under an attack that we were not trained to handle was simply too much to ask us to take on. So we dodged the doctors and the paperwork of doing a formal discharge and simply escaped.

We had already been introduced to our firefighter's help-team liaison who was assigned to escort us home. We found him outside and told him we were ready to go and we quickly left the hospital and headed back out to our firehouse in Staten Island where I hopped into my own car and drove back home. This time, I was obeying the speed limit and playing the radio to help me stay awake continuing to listening for updates. However, I did find out that they did get everyone out of the North Tower stairway B. Some of them died but most of them survived, including my friend Lt. Mickey Kross.

It was between 5 am and 6 am when I crawled into bed. I don't remember when I fell asleep or when I woke up, but I do remember the terrible nightmare. When I awoke on Wednesday, September 12th I thought that the events of September 11th had been a nightmare. But when I smelled the unmistaken odor of smoke on myself after I woke up *I knew* that crawling through the base of the North Tower and helping carry the people in the Stokes baskets wasn't a dream. It was only the part about working at Cantor Fitzgerald, the company that lost the most people in the collapse, was a dream. The 16 acre World Trade Center site really had become 25 acres of impassible disaster.

CHAPTER FOUR

Competing Realities

L ife as a firefighter placed me on the edge of two compelling
 and sometimes competing realities. In one I was a first
responder who lives to run into the scenes where chaos, destruction
and mayhem threaten the lives of others. In the other reality I was a
husband and father who lived to put a smile on my family's face and
to protect and provide for them. In the firehouse I was a part of
another family of firefighters, a brotherhood, where we understand
that whether we are together in the firehouse or inside of a flame
enveloped structure, we took a vow to protect the civilians of our
great city and to look out for each other so we could all survive to
fight another fire on another day. In the Parker house I was the
primary provider now that my wife retired from over 17 years of
service with the Red Cross where I met her. I was also the activities
coordinator, the disciplinarian, the family comedian, the handyman's
helper, the part-time backup chef and generally the man who did
whatever needed to be done. I never would have become a fireman if
I didn't have a sense of pride in what I do as well as a deep connection
to the men who served with me. But I would never trade the honor
of being a husband or a father for anything in the world. So what

happens when the demands of my brotherhood start to affect my family?

I met my wife on the city's Fallen Firefighters Memorial observance day but I never wanted to think about her having to attend one in my honor. Each October there are ceremonies held around the nation to honor the firefighters who had fallen in the past year since the last memorial. It didn't matter if the firefighter died from line of duty or non-line of duty causes, we would honor any active fireman for their service. Thousands of firemen from around the city who were off on the date of the memorial ceremony would assemble on the west side of Manhattan, near the river, in their Class A uniforms to pay their respects.

The ceremony was rarely more than an hour long, but it was understood that everyone who was not working would be filling the streets blocked off from traffic to be part of the ceremony. We would line up and listen in silence as the names of the fallen firefighters would be read. There was a bell near the person who was reading the names, and the bell would be rung five times for each name that was mentioned. The reading of the names is followed by remarks from members of leadership and then we would be dismissed to participate in a union sponsored luncheon of hot dogs, chips and beer at an off-site location.

The American Red Cross headquarters building was one of the usual places to host our luncheon. The gymnasium in the seven-story building was the perfect size to host thousands of hungry firefighters. And as my wife Judy learned as an employee there, it is the perfect place to be hit on when you are a pretty little thing who hangs out on the patio outside the building as thousands of firefighters are passing through.

She was definitely number one on the hit parade for that place, I'll tell you that much. And out of careful selection from having everyone and their brother hitting on her, she got lucky and she picked me. We started dating and one thing led to another. The next thing you know we walked down the aisle together.

Each day that I go to work there is always risk involved. Judy and our sons Jonathan and Blaze understand what I do for a living and that I can be hurt, or worse, while I'm at work. There was even one time that I accidentally rolled up onto a fire with my son Jonathan in the car. He was 5 or 6 years old at the time.

I saw plumes of black smoke coming out of the building and I parked in the driveway next to the house that was on fire. I knew that cops and fire trucks would begin arriving soon, so before leaving my car I put Jonathan in the driver's seat and tossed the car keys on the floor beneath him. I told him to blow the car horn when he saw a fireman and tell them that his dad was inside the burning building. Jonathan nodded that he understood the instructions and I locked the door and made my way towards the burning building.

I ran up the stoop and into the building through the front door. There was screaming coming from the second floor so I made my way over the stairs on my left. I crawled up the stairs towards the screaming, but before I reached the top I noticed that there were flames licking the door of the apartment where the screams were coming from. There was no way that I would be able to get inside to reach anyone. The flames were coming from the open door of the apartment just below them and I knew that the situation would continue to deteriorate quickly. There were also flames all around the stairs that were burning the hair on my arms and threatening to trap me inside the burning building as well. So I rolled back down the stairs, ran out of the door and jumped over the railing on the stoop so that I could reach the alley way besides the building that was closest to the apartment where I heard the screams.

I ran to a window that I assumed belonged to the same apartment and I saw a woman on the second story of the house who kept yelling for someone to help her children. The lick of the flames at the front door let me know that there was no way that I would be able to get into the house to get them. So I talked the woman into dropping each of her children into my arms. They were small, elementary school aged children, so I was able to quickly and effortlessly catch each one.

After I safely caught the second child and sent them away from the building with a neighbor, I was quickly joined by a sanitation worker who saw what was going on. It was perfect timing, because now it was time for the mother to jump from the window. She wasn't a big woman, but she was bigger than the small children. After several minutes of coaxing, she finally swung her legs out of the window and sat on the window ledge. With no fire trucks on the scene yet to offer a Ladder and flames quickly making their way towards the place where she sat, she finally slid off of the ledge to let gravity bring her down to where me and the sanitation worker stood.

She fell awkwardly out of the window so when she landed both she and I fell onto the ground. I think she fractured her ankle, but other than that she and her children were fine. When I made my way back to Jonathan I found a police officer sitting with him. Jonathan had done exactly what I had asked and he saw the entire thing. He had watched his father in action and was also there with me months later when I was interviewed on the Les Brown Show regarding the incident. The mother and her two children were there to tell their side of the story and they greeted me with flowers. So not only did

Jonathan get a chance to see me work, but he was able to see an outcome where the victims survived.

But what am I supposed to say to them when they know I'm leaving home to muddle through the modern hell that is now Manhattan? All of the victims did not survive this one. By the morning of September 12, 2001, every news network and major talk show on television has replayed the attacks on the towers, the pentagon and the crashed plane in Pennsylvania at least three times each hour. The Internet is filled with interviews with teary-eyed witnesses and blogs with all kinds of speculations about who was behind the attacks and what their motivations were. Every major newspaper around the country had headlines, stories and images that talked about the attacks and the victims. Our president, our mayor and other government leaders had already made public statements requesting support for the victims, words of condolence to a grieving nation and demanding justice from whomever was responsible.

Our entire nation was in mourning, New York's pride was in pieces and my wife and children were looking for family and friends who we know to live, work or play in that area. We were all looking for answers that might console our pain. In the midst of all of this I needed to leave my family to rejoin my brothers in search of the men, women and children who we knew were under the rubble. Our search had a great sense of urgency because we knew many would have already died, but we hoped there were others who were still hanging on. In a time where everything you thought you knew about what was safe is challenged, there is a natural desire to cling to the ones you feel the most responsible for protecting and hide them away from anything that might hurt them or even frighten them.

With news of the attacks being the topic of everyone's conversation and on the headline of every form of media there was no way that we could stop our boys from finding out. But after years of convincing them that there are no such things as monsters, what on earth are we supposed to do when they ask what terrorists are? Fortunately, our new home in New Jersey didn't have any buildings that were nearly as tall as the World Trade Center, but what could I say to them if they ever showed fear of heights and were too afraid to enter skyscraping buildings? How could I ever convince them that planes were safe when the most vivid images in all of our minds are of the tail end of planes protruding from the side of buildings? And what was I supposed to tell them if the body of someone they knew was pulled from a steel and concrete grave at Ground Zero?

I didn't know how to answer any of these questions. So when I got up on September 12 and I saw my kids I told them that I was alright and that I was going back into Manhattan with a few friends of mine. I hugged and kissed my family good-bye and I went to my best friend's house to get out of my house before my family had the chance to ask me the questions that I couldn't even answer for myself. Besides, as a fireman I'm trained to take action and make unsafe environments safe again, not to sit back and analyze how the environment became unsafe in the first place. The analyzing is for others to do after the main work was done. Right now was still the time for action.

Phil Petti was my best friend and a newly promoted lieutenant who had attended *Proby School* with me and was on the same squad with me back in those early days. We both got our first assignments in Manhattan-I went to mid-town and he went downtown. Years later, we both transferred into Brooklyn Ladder 148 and served together for about 10 years before he was promoted. He was a sharp guy and he definitely deserved the promotion. But with the promotion came a transfer to a new firehouse in need of a lieutenant. This meant that we didn't see each other as often as we did when we were in the same firehouse, but it didn't stop us from being friends. So the morning after Dante's Inferno lands in Manhattan and the FDNY issues a total recall to every fireman in the city and calls the nation to immediately be put on full alert, I naturally wanted to go check on him.

When I got to Phil's house I found his wife, his brother who was a Brooklyn firefighter, Phil's mother and even Phil's father, but no Phil. He didn't come home the night before and none of them had heard from Phil since the collapse of the towers. He was the covering lieutenant on Ladder 12 on the morning of September 11th. His selfless decisions saved half of his company while they were operating in 3 World Trade Center's Marriott Vista Hotel. They were anxious for news but still afraid of what the news might say. The words they spoke were always filled with optimism but the lines on their foreheads, their swollen crimson eyes and the waste basket full of tissue told another story.

"Don't worry," I consoled them, "We're going to find Phil. We'll get him. Don't you worry!"

It was already difficult to do search and rescue when you knew that there were complete strangers who needed your help. But now that I knew that my best friend Phil may still be out there, I had a much more personal reason to get back out to *The Pile* as soon as possible. It was time to go back.

FDNY policy is that once you have been hospitalized you are automatically put on medical leave so that you can fully recover before you return to work. Although it makes sense to assume that if a fireman has been in a situation that was dire enough to land him in the hospital that it would be best for him to fully heal before returning to work, I had absolutely no intention of sitting around at home hiding behind some medical leave while there were still people praying to be rescued. So I called up the medical officer and requested to be taken off of medical leave so I could report for duty. The lack of surprise in his voice made me imagine that I was not the first person to call in that day with the same request.

My next phone call was to my firehouse. The day before I had to go to my firehouse before going to Manhattan because I was on vacation and didn't have my gear with me. But this time I had my gear with me and I was not interested in taking the long scenic route to my Staten Island firehouse before heading over to Manhattan, so I called them and told them where I was going so they could make a record of it and drove to Manhattan for the first time since the attacks.

As I approached the area that would soon be known as Ground Zero, I quickly noticed how much more organized everything seemed compared to the day before. They had cordoned off the area blocks away, from Canal Street down (about a fourth of a mile away) and there were now staging areas for security, military and police. The tunnel and the subway were closed to make sure that no one interfered with the search and rescue efforts. None of this surprised me, because the day before I saw the chiefs of the various first responder agencies working together to put them into place. What I didn't expect was to see what the civilians had organized.

After I found a place to park my car I grabbed my gear and started walking up towards the nearest barricade so I could make my way up to Ground Zero and report for duty onsite. As I approached the barricade I saw Asian, Latino, Caribbean, African-American and Caucasian men, women and children of all ages standing in a silent crowd and holding signs that featured a picture and name with the words, "did you see this person? Please call..." underneath. Some of the signs also included the floor number that the person worked on and the type of position they worked-whether they were executives, executive assistants or window cleaners, there were people there to represent each one of the World Trade Center's victims. In addition to the signs that people were holding, there were thousands more signs posted on ash covered lamp posts, buildings and even on the physical barricade. Others who weren't holding signs were holding lit candles and photographs of the loved ones that they were holding vigil for. Several were whispering barely audible prayers as I approached.

When I came closer several people turned to hug me and I noticed that other first responders passing through the barricade, either to leave Ground Zero or to go out to it, were also being received with hugs, pats on the back and sometimes solemn applauses of appreciation. They were waiting patiently with hope of receiving news of their loved ones. As I walked past them and cleared the barricade I felt a lump rise in my throat as I realized that while a few of them would receive good tidings, many of them would never be able to see their loved ones alive again. As I pushed this thought out of my mind, a picture of my best friend Phil came to mind. I shook my head and took a deep breath so I could once again focus on the task at hand. This kind of negative thinking was not going to make me effective during the search and rescue process, so I needed to shake it off quickly.

The path leading up to Ground Zero was much more defined on Wednesday, September 12th than it had been on the day before. All of the firefighter rigs, ambulances and civilian vehicles were piled on the side of the street into neat piles like used up wrecks in a well maintained junk yard. Although I knew many of the rigs were brand new and even the older ones were always meticulously detailed to look like new, they all looked like dirty rubbish that was crushed, burned, destroyed and now discarded. In one day the FDNY lost over 90 pieces of major equipment, including Hook and Ladder, Engine and Rescue Company vehicles. That is more equipment than most major city fire departments have in their entire inventory. Although I had been there the day before, I could hardly believe the amount of destruction I saw before I even reached the buildings that received the hijacked planes. The damage had crept out blocks away from the location where the planes made impact.

The first things I noticed as I finally approached Ground Zero were the two footpath bridges that once connected the North and South towers. One was completely destroyed in a couple of fires but the other was still intact. And by "intact," I mean that it was utterly destroyed, but still in one piece. It may be a random thing to notice under the circumstances, but after walking a few blocks past piles of utterly destroyed vehicles and approaching a site where it looked like a team of wrecking balls had recently had a party, there was something about seeing that intact footpath bridge that barely survived obliteration that gave me a glimmer of hope that I would be able to find more survivors-ideally human survivors.

Everyone's job on Tuesday, September 11th was either search and rescue or to put out fires, but with most of the major fires put out by Wednesday, September 12th, we started forming rescue and recovery teams. We couldn't simply leave Ground Zero in piles of broken glass, concrete and steel, so now we were forming bucket brigades to move everything and everyone we found away from the site piece by piece. To do this we formed incredibly long human chains by standing shoulder to shoulder and passing buckets of debris from the top of piles out to the perimeter of the site where it was either hauled off to the nearest dump or kept to be analyzed or possibly returned to the company or individual who owned it. Every once and a while they would find human remains and directed us to move away from where we were standing so we would not desecrate their bodies.

"No, no, no," they would yell, "don't stand there!"

I think God made me stupid for a reason at that point because most of the time when I heard someone yell at me to step aside and away from a body I didn't even realize that I was near a body-I didn't know what I was looking at. Everything was covered in gray ash and dust so there was no blood to be seen anywhere. The smell of burned fabric, rubber, paper and flesh permeated the entire area so it's not like a particular smell could stand out enough to let me know that I had found someone. I believe that God knew who could handle identifying bodies and who couldn't. I was in the camp that he allowed to be ignorant so that I could keep working. Since I knew I had problems identifying bodies, I always stepped as gingerly as I could in my thoroughly sweat soaked 80 lbs. plus of gear.

We worked silently to find the people who were still alive. We had already found people who were trapped in crevices when the building fell and we anticipated, or hoped, that we would find more people in similar situations. We also listened for PASS (Personal Alert Safety System) alarms that were going off. The alarms were attached to firefighter air tanks and were designed to go off when the person stopped moving. The ear piercing sound was heard coming from every direction on the first day and the sheer volume of alarms going off simultaneously made it difficult to focus in on one PASS and find the firefighter it was attached to. But as time went on the shrieking sounds started to fade as the batteries began to die, or when the device got wet or was simply crushed in the unstable rubble.

If I had still been in my old Manhattan firehouse that I was assigned to when I first started my career, I would have been one of the first men on the scene and one of the dozens who were crushed when the Towers collapsed. It could have been me under thousands of pounds of concrete praying desperately for a cadaver dog to find me or for a fireman to wander over to my pile and dig me out. And although it obviously wasn't me who was in that situation, I just knew that many of the men who were in that situation were men I had played softball with at the FDNY vs. NYPD competitions, or ate dinner with in the firehouse, or sat next to in a rig on our way out to a call. Some of them were even the same men I would have words with and go back and forth like big brothers and little brothers who live to cause each other grief but will turn around and give their life for you-literally.

The conversation between Engine guys and Truck guys is always about which end of the station was better.

"We're the big guys and you're the little guys."

"Cheese eaters!"

"You're the bone heads."

There is always an attitude like one is the older brother and the other is the younger brother. So everything in the firehouse is a competition. There would be an annual softball game or any sport. It didn't matter. There was always a competition. So once we had enough players, we hosted our first annual roller hockey game with Engine versus Truck.

We made sure that everyone who wanted to play had a chance to play. If you didn't have a pair of skates we would get a pair for you. We made sure there were enough people on each team and we had a lot of fun. Truck won by the way.

This is the Ladder Company 148 and Engine Company 282's first annual roller hockey game in Boro Park, Brooklyn on 53rd St. and Fort Hamilton Parkway. Boro Park has one of the city's few roller hockey rinks and it has been around since the 40's. This park was actually dedicated to being a roller hockey park. There are skateboard parks and there are parks for basketball, but this one was dedicated to roller hockey. People used to play on softball fields or any open place with asphalt. I never had hair on my legs from sliding off the concrete from the time I was 8 years old up to the age of 18. We didn't play on grass. We played on concrete and asphalt.

The plan was that after we went out to have a lot of fun at the hockey game we would go to Rocco's Italian Cafeteria and get a few tables set up to feed all 20 of us. Even the guys who came out to watch and didn't play were going to eat with us. It was only a few blocks away and everyone who knows anything about Brooklyn knows that Rocco's is *the place to go* for great Italian and it has been for at least 30 or 40 years.

While we were there we had a few bottles of beer. Some may have had wine or coffee. It was real nice. It was in the afternoon, maybe about 3 o'clock. At that time, guys started heading out to go home. Most of these guys lived in Staten Island so they wanted to beat the traffic. I didn't rush off. I was actually one of the last guys to leave. Gary was there with me.

And while we were in there, 85 Truck pulls up with a big time tower ladder from Staten Island. They were taken out of service for the day so they could drive all the way from their Staten Island quarter to *The Rock* between Manhattan and Queens and then go back home, but they decided that they were going to stop at Rocco's. This was no problem because it was on the way. You get off the highway on the Fort Hamilton Parkway exit and Rocco's is right there. They parked the truck across the street from Rocco's near a bus stop that was maybe a half block away. It wasn't directly in front of the building but you could see the truck from the front window.

In situations like this, the junior guy in the rig is usually assigned to stay inside the rig and safeguard it while the others pick up food to go back to quarters and relieve the company that was covering the firehouse in their absence. But that is not what they did. These salty old hair bags decided that every one of them was going to go in there and sit down and have a lunch break like firemen *never* do. To make it worse they were sitting with their backs up against the window with nobody looking at the rig. All six of them had their back to the rig. This includes the chauffeur, the officer and the four men. Not one of them cared about their rig.

Gary and I were both chauffeurs so we knew the drill and we knew that this was not supposed to happen like this. So I decided that if none of them went out to the rig by the time I left that I was going to do something. Gary shrugged it off and said that there was nothing we could do, but I was determined that it couldn't go down like this. So Gary left and I left, but when I left I walked towards the rig instead of my car.

Rigs don't have keys. They have a safeguard switch underneath the seat with buttons and batteries that get it started. Only firefighter chauffeurs would know where it is and of course I knew exactly where it was. When I looked in the truck I saw that all the coats, all the helmets, all the masks and all their tools were in there. I threw the switch on and I got in the rig and I left. The firemen in the restaurant didn't even see me leave. I took this truck with a 95 ft. tower ladder and they didn't even see it leaving. I drove a few blocks and took a right, drove a couple more blocks and took a left. I went by this railroad cut and parked it right under a tree that hid the vehicle really well.

I got off the rig and I ran because my car was now parked down the block from the restaurant and I had to get back. I ran right past the restaurant and they were still eating with their backs up against the window. They still didn't know that their rig was missing. It must have taken me at least eight minutes to run from the where I left the truck back up to the restaurant, so that means it was over eight minutes since any of their crew of six turned to check on the rig. So I got in my car and I drove home. I laughed the entire way there.

I couldn't wait for each one of them to leave that restaurant with their mouths wide open when they realize that their truck was missing. I wasn't there to see it, but I imagine that they would have walked around in different directions to look for it and use their radios to talk with each other and relay information. I knew that it would take them quite some time to find the fire truck. They didn't want to call the chief because they weren't supposed to be there. They didn't want to call the police, but somehow they waived down a police car and made them drive around until they found it. It had to take about an hour.

A few hours later I ended up back in my firehouse. I don't think I was working that night, but for whatever reason I ended up back there again. Both the Engine and Truck were out on a call so there was no one else in the firehouse other than an officer. As soon as I walked in I heard, "Parker, come up to the office."

"Yeah. What's going on?" I knew that I wasn't working so I didn't expect much and just went up to the office.

"You take any fire truck today?" He asks.

I looked right at him, "you know, yup. I sure did." He thought that I was going to give some excuse or lie. I don't lie. I just told him that I did. I explained that these guys didn't do what they were supposed to do. I could have denied it because nobody saw me take it and no one could prove anything but I didn't see the point in lying.

"You know, I've got chiefs calling. Everybody's calling and it took them forever to find it. Their stuff was missing from the rig..." and I knew right away that he was making up stuff at this point. I knew that no one had taken their masks or any of their gear. But he continues on his rant, "all of this shit is coming down and I'm the one who has to deal with what you started."

"Look," I said, "I'm not working. So whatever you want to do." I gave him one of those looks that said that I just didn't care. I knew he was lying about having equipment missing from the truck so that he could make me feel bad, but I was not interested in any of the drama.

"You know something..." I start just as he interrupts me.

"They're going to press charges and you are going to be responsible for replacing all the stuff that is missing from the truck..." he just keeps going on and on about all the terrible things that will allegedly happen and cascade down on his head.

I turn around and I said, "You know, every fire house officer's office is filled with volumes and volumes of rules, regulations, charts, codes and all kinds of books that would make you think that you're in a law library, but each book is in relation to the fire department. Anything they need to know regarding their job is in one of those books. If they come after me, that's fine. But the shit's going to fall down on them because I'm sure that in one of those books it says that your rig should not be left unattended and not safeguarded by a member at any time. Not to mention that they didn't tell the dispatcher where they were, so there were multiple codes that they broke before I even showed up. So if they want to play the games of pressing charges against me, they are going to have to own up to what they did first. But whatever happens is fine by me, because I did take the rig. So if you want to slap me on the wrist, just do what you need to do."

He turns red like a tomato and he is furious.

"Just get the hell out of here! Get out of here!"

And that was the end of that. Nothing happened and it turned out that nothing was actually stolen from the rig. All the stories about it started to spread and we all knew that they disrespected their own company by leaving it there. After that there were several times that I took detail assignments at 84 Truck which was just down the block from 85 Truck. Each time I was in 84 Truck someone would ask me if I really took the truck from 85 Truck. When I was asked, I never denied it. They all thought it was funny and I thought it was hilarious.

"No way! You didn't really do that."

"Yes, I did! What's the big deal? I knew they'd find it...eventually. I just taught them a lesson that they shouldn't leave their rig unguarded. That's all that was."

I would never do anything to put anybody's life in jeopardy. There was a fire truck in their firehouse covering the area and they were off the air. So it's not like I would have made them late to a call because someone else was taking their calls. So there was no harm and no foul, I just wanted them to give the rig the respect it deserves. It's about honor and living up to the title of being New York's "Bravest." It took years for other salty firemen and officers to teach me and I was passing along what I learned so that they could be even better firemen than they already were.

CHAPTER FIVE

The List

Many of those men who trained me and many of those men I helped train in my own unique way were the same men I was working tirelessly to find. These were not just random people who we were recovering, these were my brothers too.

I spent almost the entire day on the bucket brigade passing five gallon buckets full of debris. The slow and steady stream of buckets continued 24 hours a day and moved through the hands of hundreds of rescue and recovery personnel including firefighters from all over the country, police officers from hundreds of cities, Port Authority police, N.Y.C. sanitation workers, military personnel from all branches of service and even priests, pastors and other clergymen who were ever present. We were all strangers who, in the face of terrorism designed to steal our hope, banned together to give hope to the mothers, fathers, husbands, wives and children who waited for news about their loved ones.

When we did manage to uncover someone, everyone in the area would stop whatever they were doing. The giant grapplers stopped picking up mounds of debris that was too heavy for humans to pick up. The trucks stopped moving. The generators were turned off.

Everything on that sixteen acre site stopped. It would be completely silent. I would immediately begin to pray for the newly found soul and I would keep praying as I waited for a retrieval basket carrying a body bag and an American flag that I would help pass to the people who were releasing the person's body from the ground.

There were some people on the rescue team who could precisely identify the exact type of human tissue discovered and could use the angle and position where it was found to help us determined where the rest of the body should be. They would use hand held Global Positioning System devices to mark the area, while respectfully protecting its contents and instruct us to move out of the way so that the experts could carefully and painstakingly dig around the area to fully release the body from the Tower's encompassing grip. And if the fallen person we discovered was a firefighter and we were able to read the company number on the helmet, turnout gear or anything else on the person, the chief-in-charge would call the members company and a detail of men from the fallen brother's firehouse would soon arrive to take out their own in a stokes basket covered with an American flag. It was always quick. A lot of guys were already there and they knew the logistics of it. We would wait in a line from deep down inside the debris field all the way out in any which pathway we could. The fallen fireman would be carried by his firehouse brethren to the top of the hill and wait for an ambulance for his final ride home.

After a while we all acknowledged that this was no longer a search and rescue as it became a total recovery. The area started to have that unmistakable rotting stench of decaying flesh and we knew that it wasn't likely that we were going to find anyone else alive. Although we knew it wasn't likely, it still didn't stop us from having hope that just maybe someone found some water, a pocket of air, or something in there that can help them hold on long enough for us to reach them. You always hear about miraculous survival skills that help people beat the odds, but no one ever came out and said, "Hey, we found somebody. We got somebody over here." As the hours and days dragged on and no new living bodies were found the new reality gradually began to set in. No one else was coming out of Dante's Crushed Inferno alive.

After hours of working on site at Ground Zero, it wasn't unusual for firemen to go back to their firehouses to get something to eat, get some rest or simply be relieved by someone else reporting for duty on the next tour, or work shift. So when it was my turn to leave Ground Zero and head to my firehouse in Staten Island, I still had to walk through the same barricades full of people holding vigil that I had passed earlier when I started my tour. Many of the same people I had seen earlier were still sitting there in the dust hopping to learn that their loved ones' lives were spared. But from what I had seen over the course of the day, I knew that, at best, they could only hope to receive the bodies of their loved ones if we could positively identify them. As hard as it was for me to watch the bodies of innocent people being recovered from the wreckage it was even harder for me to look into the eyes of people who reached out to hug me and applaud me for being part of the team who was looking for their loved ones. It wasn't until I was back at the firehouse that I learned that there were even more difficult challenges ahead.

It was while I was in the firehouse that I learned just how much anxiety a piece of paper could produce. Every so often each firehouse would post an updated version of something we simply referred to as "the list." It was supposed to be written record of all of the firemen who were reported as missing from their firehouse or who were confirmed to be either injured or deceased in the wake of the attack. Although the firehouses were always big on keeping accurate records, you have to remember that the attacks occurred at the exact time that the evening tour ends and the day tour begins-we call it the change of tours. This means that it was difficult to know for sure which evening tour guys had already gone home for the day and which ones were already relieved by a replacement and who exactly was their replacement. It was a mess.

At the change of tours there are a lot of things that can take place. If a fireman had somewhere that he really needed to be around 9 am, he might call a fellow fireman who was scheduled to relieve him and ask that the new guy come in early.

"I have to go take my kids to school today and then help my brother fix his car, can you come in an hour before me?"

So let's say you're getting out at 9 o'clock in the morning but your relief comes in at 8 o'clock. Sometimes your relief may even come in at 7 o'clock because they want to make sure that they won't get caught up in traffic. In fact, it is completely normal for replacements to come in at least an hour before the tour officially changes, so many of the guys who were schedule to work from 9 am to 6 pm were probably in their firehouses by 8 am and most likely would have been part of the crew to respond to the attacks, but that's not an exact science. Because if one of the evening tour guys who was supposed to get off at 9 am was still in the firehouse and heard that a plane crashed into the World Trade Center, I wouldn't be surprised if he decided to jump on the rig and go out with the crew because he knew this would be a big one and that more hands would be welcomed. No fireman ever wants to miss the big one...I'm just certain that none of them knew it would be quite this big or that it might come down on top of them.

To add to the confusion about which firemen were working, we have something called a "mutual exchange" where you might trade workdays with someone else. So let's say Bobby's baby girl had a doctor's appointment at 11 am on September 11th and she cried crocodile tears for him to make this one. He might have contacted another firefighter and asked if he could switch days with him so Bobby could make it home in time to hold and comfort his little girl at the doctor's office. Although the official books would say that Bobby was working, there was probably a note in the journal at the house watch desk of the firehouse that said James from the firehouse down the street was filling in for Bobby instead. It's easy for things like that to get overlooked the first couple times that the firehouse chiefs are doing roll call and looking for their men. So this means the chief may be out there walking past James and looking for Bobby when Bobby didn't even show up that day. But who's to say that when Bobby heard about what was going on downtown that he didn't turn around and run out there as soon as he could, even though he wasn't officially on duty. Firemen do things like that because we are all just a little off anyway. How else could you explain why we run into burning buildings for a living while everyone else is running out?

Here's an example of what I mean by firemen being a little different and making it difficult to track them. There was an early evening fire on Watts St. in downtown Manhattan close by the Holland Tunnel entrance. The call came in at the change of tours where a guy physically relieved another guy by pulling him out of the riding seat with the door open and the truck moving and tells him, "nah, I'm going-you're out of here." He grabs him and throws him out. The guy that rode off in the truck was killed along with two other firemen and a few more firemen in the rig were injured. In a matter of moments, the guy who was relieved was saved just because his replacement physically took his spot at the last minute. It happens. If you take a few seconds longer to get into gear than your replacement does, he will relieve you and send you on your way. With so many instances like that, it's hard to tell who is missing in the ruble, who simply passed out on a cot at the nearest firehouse on their way home, who took over a shift for someone else or who was already home with their family.

That's not the only reason things were a little confusing. For one of the first times in the history of the FDNY, all of these companies from upstate New York and New Jersey, mostly from New Jersey and Long Island, came in with their rigs and their crews to man the firehouses that belonged to all the companies there were out at Ground Zero. Although it was great to have someone there to cover the regular gamut of daily calls about fires, car accidents and other emergencies around Manhattan, Brooklyn, Queens and Bronx, but these guys from upstate New York and New Jersey didn't know anything about our protocols for running our firehouses. They didn't know how to navigate their way around the city like we did and they didn't know how to deal with the kinds of emergencies that we were used to. If you work in a city where the tallest building has about 8-10 floors, what are they going to do when they have a report for a fire on the 26th floor? They were not conditioned to carry up to 80 lbs. worth of gear and equipment up that many flights. What do they know about how to approach a rear tenement building that requires you to go through one building in order to enter it? They were not even used to using the same type of equipment that we used because it wasn't necessary where they came from.

"These are the tools you'll use, this one you're never going to use-so throw this away. Get back two of these and none of those."

We appreciated them for stepping up and being our new millennium minute men, but you're only good at what you do and they were not used to what we did. This was especially true for the firemen from New Jersey who came from cities where there were no high-rises at all and they spent more time responding to car accidents than fires. They had about five minutes to learn what they needed from the native firefighting companies in between their tours of work down at Ground Zero. It was a mess in the firehouses. I sincerely thank and commend them for stepping up putting their lives on the line to fill the giant void at a time that our department most desperately needed help. Again true American patriotism prevails.

Each time I saw the list it seemed to bring about more questions than answers. Some lists had 200 names on it and sometimes it was 300 or 500 names long. We didn't really pay much attention to how long the list was because we were too busy looking for our friends and family-many firemen had their fathers, brothers, sons and nephews serving in the brotherhood as well. Was this list the "official list"? Had all of the facts been collected? Are they sure that this person was dead or was it possible that they found a piece of his gear and didn't realize that he dropped it as he was carried off to the hospital and he was really in intensive care somewhere and overlooked because his name was written on the paperwork incorrectly?

Then it just went from bad to worse when I realized that there were 45 guys on the list that I knew. Some of them I knew really, really well. And some of them I just played softball with or I shared a tour in their house on a detail with them, "oh, I didn't know you were a musician. Play that song for me again." But I remembered the guy because I had seen him more than once. And the guy says,

"I just got promoted."

"Oh, you got promoted! How did that happen?!"

"Yeah, finally hit the books working in the battalion."

You know, I play soccer, I play ice hockey, we set up road trips, baseball games and bus trips...all kinds of stuff. And you're always running into guys. Guys you went to *Proby School* with but you hadn't seen in a while...it was just horrible to see so many of their names together on this list. After a while you don't even want to look at the list because you know too many guys on it.

And after everything I had seen at Ground Zero, at the barricade vigils on the perimeter of the area and after skimming through a list of hundreds of men who had lost their lives as I searched for the ones I knew, I still had to go home each day and face my family and friends. What on earth was I supposed to tell them? Was I supposed to tell them the unadulterated truth? Should I tell them that being in Ground Zero was horrific. I truly know now what Dante's Inferno was. I know what it is. I saw it. I walked through it. I breathed and swallowed it in. It's embedded in my DNA, seared in my memory for ever. I lived it. Ground Zero looked like a nuclear holocaust. It looked like Hiroshima or Nagasaki in August of 1945 when the Allies dropped atomic bombs over the cities to force Japan to surrender and end World War II. I mean, the cars in the street were all crushed, some reduced to the size of a crushed beer can. We were looking at skeletons of cars and trucks and fire trucks and police cars and buildings. We didn't have access to any water on the street because the water mains collapsed and the sewer lines were broken. The power lines were cut. I couldn't even imagine it. We were putting major building fires out as a secondary concern; a much later reaction and response never before done by the city's Bravest.

Should I tell them about the hours I spent going through some of New York's largest hotels forcing thousands of doors open in search of people who may, or may not, have been in their rooms when a huge chunk of the Big Apple collapsed? Fortunately, in most of the rooms I found dust coated, neatly made beds. But even in these rooms there was more work to be done-the window of each room usually had shattered shards of half inch wide glass that was precariously attached to the window sill and simply waiting for a tremor or gust of wind to launch it through the air like a dart hurling towards a dart board. My detail partner and I would have to take the delicate and dangerous task of removing each piece from the inside of the room. One slip and you and your teammate holding you half out the window would be added to the list, not to mention who else you could injure or kill down below. Scores of fire department teams were precariously scrambling all over the place. And every single door was forced open and was broken. I was thinking "who broke in all these doors? " There was probably nobody in them, but you had to check! Check the closets, check under the bed, check the closets, we would check everything! God forbid you forgot to check something.

Or maybe I should tell my family and friends how, for the first time in my 17 years of service to the FDNY, I received detail assignments that were never before necessary-like installing cameras on what may have been the 30th floor of the Millennium hotel so that every move on the premises could be recorded? Or how there were FBI agents and people from all different government branches, both military and non-military, who were crawling the site alongside me and all conducting their own business of investigation.

I certainly didn't want to tell them about how we lost the best of the best in that killing field. All the rescue companies, all the squad companies, all the trucking companies in Manhattan-these guys were high-rise experts and some of the first men on the scene and to go up into the towers to help people out seconds before the entire building collapsed on top of them and their equipment.

As much as I didn't want to go home and talk about all the lives that were lost, there was one family that I had promised to follow-up with. I had already told my best friend Phil Petti's family that I would find him for them. I wasn't the one who found his body, it was someone else. I had only found Phil's name on the list. I knew that he had served in one of the units that would have been early on the scene, but I had hoped that maybe he had miraculously survived. Since this didn't happen, the only thing left for me to do was to stay by his family's side as they prepared to say final goodbye's and lay him to rest. We all went to Phil's funeral, but it was all a dismal somber blur-another living nightmare.

CHAPTER SIX

Home Training

September 11th completely changed what I thought I knew about the world, what I thought I knew about being a firefighter and what I thought I knew about myself. I was never under any delusions that there weren't evil forces at work in the world-I learned that from what my father's life as a Merchant Marine and a NYPD police officer had shown me.

My father was born Salvator Panasedi in the Lower East Side of Manhattan. The area was known as "Little Italy." Both of his parents, and both of my mom's parents, were Sicilian. He changed his name in 1947 after World War II to Charles Parker. My uncle Raymond also changed his last name to Parker. He got the name from his god father, Charles Gazetta, who worked in a small upholstery shop in Bay Ridge. He did it because of the prejudice against Italians and other minorities. There were also a lot of Jews who changed their name around that time. So he went into the phone book and picked out "Parker," a very generic name, and so went from Salvator Panasedi to Charles Parker.

He was a first generation Italian-America who was raised by his mother Mary and his mother's parents along with his brother Raymond. He was an excellent athlete; other than his life being interrupted by WWII, he had a great opportunity to play collegiate football as well as baseball with a promising sports future. I guess my dad decided to become a cop sometime after he came out of World War II. He was a mariner in the Merchant Marines who transported oil, ammunition, tanks, soldiers, or whatever was needed to support the invasion of France. He was a crew member aboard Liberty Ship.

He saw a great many of his fellow sailors get killed. During his many crossings of the north Atlantic he witnessed a lot of ships blow up right in front of him. His ship was always at risk of attack from submarines, mines, aerial attacks and even the natural elements of the high seas. He lived through that. He said to me that when they don't tell sailors where they're going the sailors automatically knew they were going to be part of the invasion. He said when he woke up that morning in the sunlight and he saw thousands of ships all in a line, or in columns as he called them. Whatever they did, he made many trips, but the invasion of France was the big one and he said that he remembers the ship right in front of his exploding from either hitting a mine or being hit by a torpedo. He said, "You could have read the fine print of the New York Times." The death and destruction he saw came at a time when he knew we were at war. My exposure to September 11th came as a total surprise!

When he came out of the war he didn't go to college, he didn't go to play football, he didn't do any of this stuff that he thought he was going to do. He came of age at the tail end of the depression, so after a short career as a mariner, or sailor, who traveled the world and being constantly exposed to danger, he decided that a city job may give him a good foundation because it allowed him to stay in the community that he loved and offered a moderate amount of protection from the layoffs that were so prominent at the time. Between the options of becoming a policeman, a fireman or a sanitation worker, the police department's career suited him best. The 64th precinct in Bay Ridge Brooklyn was his home for all of his 23 years of service. Besides, most of the trades at the time were mob controlled and those who weren't were run by unions that only hired family members and close friends of people already in the union.

My older brother, Charlie, would say, "Look, they're building this new thing in the city. I can get a job. Johnny Wiseguy's brother is going to get me in." Everyone knew that some of the people in those unions didn't really work anyway because the mob controlled union would cover them. Thirty people sign up for work and only twenty two people show up. The others, who didn't show up, probably went to run the numbers, gamble at racetracks and start drinking and smoking and doing other things that made the mob more money. My father didn't want us to be surrounded by that. He figured we'd be the ring leaders of that nasty circus after a while. He was smart enough to know the personalities of his children and he kept a watchful eye over us.

"Look, the city job is a great foundation," he often told us.

"You can have your house. You'll have your crappy car to go to work. You'll have your house, a couple of kids and your dog and you'll never be more than a month behind all your bills. How bad is that?"

That's the way he figured it.

He was so excited when he learned that I was going to be a firefighter.

"Wow, that's great," he had exclaimed.

We didn't know too many firefighters because, similar to union positions at that time, it was a nepotism thing where the family and close friends of current firefighters were often introduced to the culture, the tools, the trade secrets and even the chiefs and other leaders who made the key hiring decisions well before they needed the information-so when it was time apply for the job they practically had a guaranteed position. So when I officially became a firefighter, in spite of not having a *rabbi* as the person who is often called in to help you get in, my father was exceptionally proud.

I too have always had a sense of pride in having the greatest job on earth by being part of New York's "Bravest." September 11th reminded me that we didn't have that title simply because it sounded good, we earned it. By September 13th, two days after the city as we knew it collapsed, my new routine of calling in to my firehouse and heading into Manhattan was already starting to become ingrained in my system. It didn't matter that I was still scheduled to be on vacation, it didn't matter how much my muscles ached from lugging my soggy 80 plus pounds of gear across the 25 acre site for hours at a time and it didn't matter how heavy my heart felt each time another body was recovered or a new list was released in the firehouse-there was still work to be done and I was not going to let anything keep me from it. There were too many people holding vigil at the barricades and too many more in different parts of the nation, and in some cases around the world, who were anxious to receive the remains of their loved ones so they could be placed to rest.

By now, hope of finding anyone alive had been replaced with the hope that we could at least find the remains of everyone who was in or near the building so that we could return them to their families.

Even this was quite the task. When someone is on the 85th floor when a glass, steel and concrete avalanche falls to the ground there is no guarantee that the same person will be a good candidate for an open casket funeral. Our primary goal was to find them so that they could be positively identified and laid to rest. Our secondary goal was to remove all of the completely destroyed debris so that the men, women and children who lived, worked and played in the area surrounding 25 acre site could soon return safely. Even the stock market was still closed.

In order to get the job done we formed more bucket brigades. There were dozens of bucket brigade lines all around the site that snaked across the heaps of wreckage during our recovery efforts. I wasn't the only person who was getting used to the routine. Everything seemed to flow much more easily. The task ahead of us never became any easier, but my confidence in our ability to tackle it certainly did. It was obvious the chiefs knew what they were doing and they adapted to this ever changing dangerous situation very well.

After my experience with viewing the lists in the firehouses the day before, I decided that I would rather take short breaks out near the site than go into another firehouse and face another updated list. I simply could not take it anymore. I took a break and laid in the atrium of a big glass building that was part of the American Express headquarters. It resembled a big broken inverted fishbowl. The glass was shattered and the palm trees that once served as accent pieces for the classy main lobby were now wrecked pieces of timber. While I was lying on the floor and just taking a breather I saw three firemen walk right into the lobby. They were pristine GQ firefighters in brand new gear with everything ready to rock and roll. Now that we were three days into our recovery efforts, even the *probys* just out of school had collected more filth than that on their gear. I looked at them and said, "Boy, where the hell have you guys been?" I've never wanted to take back any words, more than those.

The trio had just driven non-stop from Seattle, Washington and were ready to work. They had been driving since Tuesday, September 11th and they were just now arriving on Thursday. When they asked me if leaving their car in New Jersey was okay, I told them it was fine and not to worry about it. Then I told them where they could find the chief-in-charge. Meanwhile, I couldn't tell you where their car was, but I could tell you that I felt like a horse's ass for what I had said. These guys were the real deal, real confined space rescue men who drove 2,860 miles non-stop, which takes about 41 hours to drive, from their firehouse on the west coast to the east coast just to back us up. If I never learned anything else about them, I learned that they were true warriors.

In the firehouse, the chiefs are always the chiefs. They are the ones who usually have 20 years or more of experience. They are the first ones into the fire and the last ones out. It takes a real leader to convince men to run into a burning building with you and trust you to make all the calls. The rest of us are the pawns. We follow the chain of command and do what the chief says without questioning. We act based on our trust of our chief. But at a moment's notice any of us can become warriors. These three firefighters who made the decision to jump in their cars and drive almost 3,000 miles almost immediately after learning about the attacks are the epitome of what it means to be a warrior. They inspired me to go back out on *The Pile* and do more work.

If you would have asked me a week prior what I would have been doing on Thursday, September 13th, I would have told you that I would be either doing work around the house or working my part time job as a limo driver. As a man who lived in the depression era, my father appreciated the fact that my job's two-days on and one-day off schedule gave me the opportunity to pick up part-time work elsewhere for extra funds. You could paint houses or drive a cab or do any other side-work that didn't compete with the time you needed to be working as a firefighter. When he learned of this he said, "Boy, if I had that job!" When my father was a cop there was no such thing as moonlighting. You couldn't have another job because they figured if you did you were in the mob. You had to be doing something wrong. It was not allowed. You would get fired...I guess if your family had a business that might have been something else, but for the most part nobody did. And there was really no such thing as overtime. You just worked when you worked and received your regular pay.

My Dad was a really wise person who did not receive a formal higher education-he was self-educated. He loved to read. He read the newspaper-especially the Times. He never gambled in his life, ever. He would go to Atlantic City with my mother when the casino finally first came out. She would play the slot machine with the nickels that she saved while he would walk up and down the boardwalk. My father used to walk the neighborhood with the dog. That's it. He loved to walk. He would talk to people.

My father was very, very, very conservative. You would never know he was a cop. He didn't look like a cop, didn't act like a cop. I think I'd seen him in uniform twice in my life. When cops retire they have to turn in their badge, their gun and their black ticket book, or summons book, to their captain. When my father returned his stuff, the captain looks at him and said, "Charlie, this summons book...we haven't used these summonses in ten years."

"I haven't used them since I got them," my dad replied.

My father must have given out three summonses in 20 years. He was the kind of guy who would pull you over and give you one of those 20 minute sermons about how dangerous it is to drive like that.

"I know you were in a hurry and you have to get home, but now you're going to get a ticket. That could be a whole $7. Oh, my God, your husband will kill you."

He was that kind of guy.

"Listen, you got to take care of your family, you got to be careful, be extra, extra careful."

His major values were family and pennies. My father was born October 2nd, 1921 and those were the messages that stuck as he grew up during the depression.

"Please, take care of yourself. I don't want to go to an accident."

This is what he said and that was the kind of cop he was.

He spent most of the later years of his career in the precinct. He wasn't out there fighting crime and chronic traffic violators anymore. When you got 20 years on the force you are basically an old timer. They simply gave him one of the calmer details of the 64 precinct to do and while the captain was upstairs in his office reading the Daily News, dad was down in the basement reading his favorite paper, the New York Times. The station always held at least one desk sergeant, a captain and a cop. My dad was the one cop.

I think my dad retired in 1970. He got out at the wrong time because Mayor Lindsay gave the city workers raises in each of the two years after my dad retired. He missed it and never had a good raise in his total of 23 or 24 years of service.

With each new detail I took while I was out at Ground Zero, my thoughts kept going back and forth between the task at hand and my family. Especially when our recovery led me to find part of a mouse pad, picture frame, keys, or any other personal item, I couldn't help but think about how each person in that building had their own story. For all I knew my father may have pulled over one of the relatives of whoever used to own the comb I found in the rubble. Or maybe the person who once sat in the chair I was removing was the same person I used to run into when I visited my friend's bar, New York, New York. And when I wasn't imagining what the story was behind each person who was now in the rubble I would think about my own history and how it lead me to that moment.

I grew up in an Italian neighborhood in Brooklyn. It was called Bensonhurst. I grew up with four brothers. Charles (Charlie) was born in November of 1953 and I was born about 18 months later on July 12th 1955. Richie was born June 3rd in 1958 and my sister, Loretta, was born March 7th in 1960. I was eight years old when she died three and a half years later, just months before her fourth birthday. My youngest brother Greg was born later.

It goes without saying that my brothers and I took full advantage of the opportunity to skip out on doing homework for a while when Loretta was alive. The problem was that my sister was hospitalized before the age of one and she lived most of her life in the hospital for a grand total of almost three years. We were watched over after school by our grandmother after her backbreaking work as the neighborhood seamstress. Sometimes friends of the family would step up as well as aunts, uncles and neighbors to care for and control the three busy boys.

Dad would pick up mom every day after his tour at the station house and Mom would stand vigil by the front door for dad's arrival. Not to waste any time she would run to the car as it pulled up. Once she took her place in the passenger seat they would trek to the city to be with the only daughter they would ever have. She would have done all the housework prior and have prepared dinner for all of us ahead of time. Mom would have dinner with dad much later in the evening, well after we had been put to bed and all asleep.

Every night before they went to bed they made their rounds to hug and kiss us a goodnights sleep. Charlie was always up pretending to be asleep when they entered the bedroom that we shared. While waiting and praying for the good and encouraging news that my mom would tell him how much better she was doing while responding to a new treatment or medicine. I remained quiet and would attentively listen to my mom's sweet, loving, encouraging words. Mom and dad were always by Loretta's side at the very best expensive Manhattan hospitals that had the world's best doctors who shared all of their knowledge and were ready to try experimental treatment on that deadly blood cancer known as leukemia. When she was well enough we all would call her on the telephone to tell her how much we missed her and loved her. Loretta had but one request. She especially loved it when Charlie would whistle the officer Joe Bolton theme-song perfectly without missing a note. Ironically, officer Joe Bolton was the cop that would host the daily afternoon Three Stooges TV show. My dad, the cop, lived with the other Three Stooges at home. At the age of three she came home only two times during the summer for a few weeks. Mom and dad said she was tired and needed to go back for a little while to get her strength up is all. Loretta came home for the last time sometime after Thanksgiving but before Christmas. We all thought this was going to be the very best Christmas we ever had. The whole family would be together for the first time during Christmas. Every inch of the whole house was decorated inside and out with the greatest of lights and decoration. Christmas at our house was the number one most fantastic holiday, hands down.

Charlie and I were upstairs washing our large toy trucks in the bathtub carwash, making a watery mess all over the bathroom floor (I used to wonder why the kitchen ceiling would sometime leak) Charlie perked up and heard the very unusual early arrival of mom and dad on that cold December 19th of 1963. We had no time to mop up the mess we made in the bathroom. We both slid down the banister in a hurry because we knew that they could have only arrived home because they had brought our baby sister Loretta home with them just in time for Christmas. When dad called for the three of us to sit on the couch after he had switched off all the Christmas lights, suddenly our hearts sank. I felt like I was punched in the gut so hard I could hardly breathe. Endless shrieks, screams and tears filled the Parker house for the rest of the night.

It was many years later before I learned from my mom why we never went on a real family vacation after my sister Loretta had left us to be with the Lord. After dodging the question time after time, she revealed that my dad personally went to speak to all of my sister's doctors and asked each of them a simple question.

"If I were Rockefeller could you have provided any other treatment that could have saved my little girl's life?"

They all responded with a resounding no, no way. Everything medically possible was done for her. Dad said "fine" and thanked them all for their caring professional services and asked for the bill. He said it would take some time but he assured them that the bill would be paid in full, all the way down to the last penny. It took dad sixteen years after his little angel was in the ground to finally make that promise a reality.

A picture of my sister Loretta hung on the Italian handmade Craftex plaster wall between the living room and the dining room visible from the front porch. Dad always tipped his hat to her upon entering or exiting our home. Every day, Dad's morning prayers were recited in her presence. Every time he passed that wall he looked up at her, said hello and rubbed the Craftex wall. After many years of repeating the welcome he unwillingly and completely removed the texture of the wall rendering it flat and smooth. My darling mother, to the day of this writing in her 87th year God Bless her, wears a gold locket with Loretta's photo inside around her neck and never ever takes it off. This year just passed the 50 year anniversary of my sister Loretta's death.

Parents should never bury their children.

Many years have passed and my Christmases have never been the same. My children Jonathan and Blaze always ask me why we don't setup the Christmas tree until it's almost time for Santa. All our friends have had their trees, lights and decorations up since the first break in the weather after the Thanksgiving holiday.

"Santa's going to pass up our house if the Christmas tree isn't up and the outside lights aren't on."

"It's almost Christmas. If you don't set up the tree, were going to turn Jewish and celebrate Chanukah instead and get eight days of presents instead of one day's worth of gifts." I explained that we grew up setting up the Christmas tree and lights always after December 19th in remembrance of my sister Loretta who is celebrating in heaven. To this very day that's the way it is in the Parker household and always will be while I'm alive.

Everybody in our neighborhood worked for a living. I grew up in a Jewish/Italian neighborhood and the Irish were just on the other side in Bay Ridge, the area where my father worked, which was only about four miles away. Our neighborhood had your run of the mill laborers like the seamstresses and those who worked in sweatshops. Then you had the gangsters. Everybody's all mixed up into one space but we all had an understanding of who was who. The gangsters drove the Cadillac's and they had the money. They hung out in the 18th Avenue cafés and pool halls that sometimes doubled as bookie joints. The rest of us knew not to go near. You didn't associate with these people. You didn't walk by the areas where they hung out.

That may have been why my father preferred to work in the Bay Ridge precinct. Bay Ridge was different. It was mostly Irish and all the cops had to deal with in Bay Ridge was the Friday night drinking and fighting. And although he was a first generation Italian, he preferred not to have anything to do with the bad seed Italians that were in the neighborhood. Back then, the Italian gangsters only bothered themselves and didn't mess with the rest of the people.

My father didn't want us to associate with any of those people or their children. This was easy enough to do because most of them paid to put their kids into private Catholic schools and we went to public schools. I guess they thought you could buy your way to Heaven- the hypocrite personified.

My father did his best to keep us from getting involved with these people. That's why he even discouraged us from becoming police officers because he knew that we would end up dealing with them on a regular basis and maybe even earn their hatred by interfering with their business practices. But with all the energy he put into keeping us away from them, he didn't see it coming when his cousin became deeply involved in their affairs.

Since the 1930s, there have been five Italian American Mafia crime families that have been known to orchestrate all of the organized crime in the state and, in some cases, across the nation. The Gambino family is one of the families and is credited with everything from construction racketeering to money laundering and prostitution. In 1976 Gambino named his brother-in-law Paul Castellano his successor. My father's cousin Evelyn married Paul Castellano's brother.

My dad only had one brother, so he was very close to his cousins as well-including Evelyn. I saw the pictures and even I could tell that she was a very lovely lady. He had always said that she was a real nice gal. Dad and my mom went to Evelyn's wedding at the Waldorf Astoria but that was the last time my father allowed himself to be in contact with her. He had basically said, "Evelyn, I'll see ya. Have a great life. I'll never know your kids and everybody else." How could he stay in touch? He was a police officer and he couldn't risk being around Paul Castellano or anyone associated with him. He didn't cross the line. He didn't play both sides of the fence. I don't think I ever met the woman once in my life.

No one really held it against her. It was what it was. I learned about her when I saw her in the old black and white photo albums that my mom kept. They were the albums with the black backing papers and the little white corners to hold the pictures in place. My mother's had tons of photos. We'd just go through them and ask questions.

"Who's that?"

"Oh, that's Uncle Al, that's your father's cousin."

"What cousin? I don't know these cousins."

"Well, that was Castellano."

They told me that my cousin Evelyn lived in a big house somewhere on Ocean Parkway. That's all I knew.

When my mom was a young woman, she just collected everybody's photographs. She wasn't around to take them. Grandma had them and she put them in a book for her. Grandma just had them on the dresser or in a drawer.

My mother, Nancy Spitaleri, also was a first generation Italian-American. She was born in the Bronx on St. Patrick's Day in 1926. I suppose that might be why green is her favorite color. Our whole house was green or at least accented in green-with the exception of the ceilings. Even the garage was green. If we would have had a dog, he probably would have been green too. That's just how much she liked it.

She was raised in Brooklyn and had three sisters-two of which were twins. There was Anne, my Godmother, my mom, Mary and Jeanie. Her father, my grandfather, was an exceptionally gifted tailor who was known for his caring nature and generosity. Often, during the great depression, he would purchase and deliver food for needy out of work families throughout the working class community he lived in. He died of a massive heart attack at age forty nine. I am convinced that God needed another Saint somewhere else.

Nancy was just was like the mother in "Dennis the Menace" or the mom on "Leave it to Beaver," except she was much more beautiful. She also worked ten times harder than them. She must have done nine loads of laundry a day down in the cellar to have clean clothes for our family of eight-there were a total of five boys, my mom, my dad and my grandmother, "Nanny," my dad's mother, who also lived with us. After doing laundry, Nancy would hang up each individual item on the clothes line from the second floor bathroom window, then iron the clothes once they were dry, restock the dresser drawers, make all of the beds, sweep, mop and clean up the rest of the house.

Our semi-attached brick home had a cellar but not a basement. Nobody had a finished basement. The first floor held a porch, the living room, dining room and the kitchen. The second floor held three bedrooms and a bathroom, that's it. Having the eight of us in a three bedroom and one bathroom house was definitely interesting on school days. I slept on the porch on the pull-out bed or in the living room on the other pull-out bed. It was tight, that was sure, but we went to bed so late that it wouldn't matter. Whenever we were ready for bed we would pull out the bed and go to sleep. That's how we made due. I like to refer to that experience as being "character building." It never occurred to us that there could be any other way of living because this is how we grew up.

My mom was great. She would just cook and clean and do everything. She would cook the most delicious Italian meals every day, from scratch, on a minuscule budget. Everyone would love to come over to eat anything prepared by her. Whether it was day or night, guests would come. They especially loved the leftovers. Our refrigerator probably set a world record for the number of times it was opened and closed in a single day. Of all her sisters, aunts, cousins and even her mother, she was hands down the best cook in the whole family and everyone agreed.

If you were blessed to attend a Nancy Parker Christmas dinner, you would be eating a meal that took months to save for and three full days to prepare. You were surrounded with the complete set of Spode Christmas Collection dinner ware, complete with festive Christmas glasses, candlesticks adorned with red, green and gold candles, exquisite custom tablecloths and fine cut crystal wine decanters filled to the brim with imported Italian wines.

Our appetizers were fit for a king and they consisted of no less than four to five trays of black olives, green olives, Sicilian olives, Greek olives, pimento stuffed olives, celery, carrots, fresh oven roasted peppers with roasted garlic, hot and sweet stuffed cherry peppers, pepperoncini, sardines, breadstick rolled Genoa salami, rolled mortadella, rolled baloney for the kids and rolled ham-all prepared by hand. Fresh prosciutto with melon, fresh mozzarella, tomatoes and basil, fried mozzarella, homemade caponata, eggplant, sliced provolone, gorgonzola, Fontina Val d'Aosta, chunks of Parmigiano-Reggiano, asiago, ricotta salada, pecorino, Romano cheeses, American yellow and white cheese for the light weights, baked clams, homemade garlic bread with oven melted mozzarella and famously fresh crunchy hot Italian bread from Alba's bakery on 18th Ave.

After about an hour and a half of devouring the appetizers, a complete surrender ensued and guests retreated to the living room or outside to smoke while they waited for round two. This round featured Nancy's famous homemade stuffed manicotti, more wine, but no more bread to help the guests leave room for dinner. After this round guests would retreat again to loosen their belts in preparation for round three. This round included oven baked ham, mouth-watering prime rib, softball sized rice balls with raisins (for Uncle Ray) or peas that were simply to die for. There would also be fried potato croquettes, stuffed mushrooms, sweet potato mash and a lovely green salad.

And lastly, for desert (for the ones who would make room), after espresso and brown coffee (or at least that's what they always called it), honey struffolis with colored sprinkles, walnut tarts, apricot and strawberry filled cookies, store bought cannoli, trays of seven layer rainbow cookies, as well as every other Italian cookie and pastry known to man. And then there was the fruit. There was so much fruit and nuts that the table looked like a jungle exploded all over it. It was a truly wonderful dining experience that was enjoyed by all. Nancy worked that kitchen with the precision and speed of an army of chefs, waiters and bus boys and took pleasure in making sure that everyone from the youngest family member to the oldest was pampered, fully satisfied and left remembering that they were special to her.

Jonathan & Dad's Rescue

North Tower Starting to Collapse

9/11 Cars and Street Debris

Tim Duffy the WTC 9/11 Fire Biker

Ron's Helmet Identifying Where He Entered

The Mall at The WTC

Mike Wernick's Rig

Ron on Engine 76 from 100 St. in Harlem

Inside One of The Fallen Towers

3 Days Later on West St. in Front of American Express Building

Cantor Fitzgerald Mousepad

Part of the Plane That Hit Twin Towers

Parker Salutes Lady Liberty Aboard Liberty Island

Ferry When Statue Re-opened

Ron and Mickey Kross at USS NEW YORK Christening

Ron Working at Tribute as a Docent

CHAPTER SEVEN

The FDNY Journey

W e never went to a baseball game that you had to pay for. We couldn't afford that luxury. You know how we went to a baseball game? We drank milk by the gallon because they used to have those milk cartons where you save 10 coupons and then you received one ticket to some worthless Mets game. We used to drink four or five of them a day to earn those free tickets. They only had select games that you could go to. My father would take us to Mets games because they were free. That was the only way we went.

As children of Great Depression era parents, we didn't really know anyone that went on vacation. A couple of kids would go to the Catskills Mountains and other adventures, but that wasn't our thing. We used to go on day trips, like going to the beach or to Palisades Amusement Park. We'd do stuff like that. My uncle had a 28 foot boat which was like a small cabin cruiser made out of wood, but it wasn't the kind of thing you would take 10 people with you. We only did it once. Me and my brother, we'd go out on the water with my mother and my father, something like that. My uncle already had a wife and two kids of his own to fit onto the boat, so that's why when we went our parents only took me and Charlie, the two oldest.

115

My mother would take us to Bay Ridge to visit their shopping district. I remember there was a movie theater called Dyker that was right next door to the 64th precinct where my father worked. It is now known as the 68th precinct. My mom would take me and my brothers to the movies and my dad would join us later after he got off of work. Treats like that meant the world to me and my brothers.

One grandmother, my father's mother, spoke fluent Italian and perfect English. She helped my mother look after us. My other grandmother went to work in a dress factory. We didn't have any real structure in our lives. When I went to school I did whatever it was that I wanted to do and that was not always what the teacher was asking us to do. I wasn't a dummy by any means, but if I was taught how to study correctly in a structured setting, I would have done much better in school and probably achieved greater academic success. I wanted to skate through school and get a 70-the lowest grade I could possibly get without failing. I just wanted to mind my own business and get by with doing the least amount possible. I didn't like school very much at all, but I really liked athletics.

My father always had a trunk full of baseballs and bats and footballs and we always played in front of the house. During the summer we couldn't wait for our father to get off of work so we could go down to the beach. He would get off of work around 4 pm, come in the house to change his clothes and by the time he got back out to the car we were all waiting on him. About three or four times a week we would take one of our friends with us on the 18-20 minute ride down to Manhattan Beach. We would arrive around 4:30 pm while everybody was leaving and we'd stay until 6:30 when we were ready for dinner. He tried to take advantage of the opportunity to enlighten us and teach us, but we didn't want to hear his mouth. We were more interested in crashing against the waves that were always higher late in the day. Sometimes mom came with us too. It was great!

When we weren't at the beach we played in our backyard pool. We had one of those little metal pools in our backyard for as long as I could remember. I think our first pool was one of those one foot canvas ones with the little metal corners. To me it looked like a recycled army tent that the military decided to make money off of after the war. Then we got one of those little two foot metal ones. Then we got a three foot one. Then we ended up with a four foot one with a filter and all that other gear that we didn't need.

Every year we used to put it up in time for summer and then we would take it down. When it was time to take the pool out we would put all those little bolts down the side and put the things on the top and fill it with water from our hose or even borrow a neighbor's hose if we had to. As the summer ended we cleaned out the liner, undid each of the bolts on each side, rolled it up and put it in the garage.

A lot of the neighbors had pools after a while, but we were the first. Because all our friends knew that we had a pool each year our friends were always over. Often we would drag the picnic table out of the garage and the barbeque. I could play ball two blocks away at the school yard, come back, dive in the pool and hang out all day. That part of growing up was really great. But as soon as the barbecue was over the bench had to go away. And as soon as the summer was over we quickly put away the pool because we needed the parking space. It gave us more room so that it was less likely that we would hit the driveway wall that divided our driveway from the driveway of the home across from ours.

Our semi-attached brick house reached over a driveway to connect with our neighbor's house. The narrow driveway turned my brothers and me into great drivers, because our family had these big power station wagons that only gave us an inch-and-a-half on each side before we hit the brick. With a family of eight, it was simply understood that you were not supposed to break anything because funds were tight and we were not interested in paying to get something fixed. You couldn't ever borrow my father's car ever. He trained you and he would show you where everything on the car was located and how it worked, but we all knew that if you wanted to drive you would have to get your own car or borrow someone else's.

I'm not sure who should get the credit for making my older brother Charlie the best driver I have ever seen, whether it was the tight driveway, my father's training, or a combination. My brother could have easily been a winning NASCAR driver. If anybody north of the Mason Dixon Line ever had a chance, it would have easily been my older brother Charlie. Anybody who has been in a vehicle with him will tell you that. He pulled over 1,000 automotive stunts that probably should have killed us. But he never even had an accident. I have never seen anybody drive like him. He worked as a delivery boy for a nearby pharmacy and saved for two years to buy his first car at the age of 17. He bought a 2-door fastback '69 Plymouth Barracuda with a 340 engine. It was a monster car and he used to drive it like a well skilled maniac.

I will never forget the summer day that he pulled a stunt in the driveway that I never thought was possible. Because our house was attached to another one, there were two garages that were side-by-side. Ours was the one on the right. In order to get out you would have to back the car out of the garage and out towards the left so you could straighten the wheel and ride to the bottom of the driveway, up over the little hill where the stoops were and then go out onto the street. Near the street entrance there were two white columns that you needed to avoid so we couldn't make a wide turn there or you would end up hitting the columns. Well, after cleaning his always immaculate car, my brother lined up the car and I tell you he burned rubber down the whole driveway to the street. It was like we were at the race track. That rubber stayed on the concrete for three or four years.

I spent most of my time and all of my summers in the P.S. 205 schoolyard playing games like *Ringalevio, Johnny on the Pony* and *Spud* which was also known as *Balls and Guts. Balls and Guts* was a game that I made up.

We would start the game by assigning a number to each of the players. Usually the largest kid on the court would be the person to start the game because no one else would challenge him. Next, they would slam a small pink Spalding rubber ball onto the concrete ground to make it bounce up as high as possible. Sometimes the ball would reach up two or three stories into the air. While the ball was in the air, all of the players would run away to hide while the person who bounced the ball would call out a number. If your number was called you had to try to catch the ball before it touched the ground.

If you caught it on the fly, it was now your turn to bounce the ball into the air and call someone else's number. But sometimes kids would run so far away to hide that they wouldn't make it back in time before it bounces. If you didn't catch it, you chased it, grabbed it and yelled "freeze." All players had to immediately stop running and hiding while you picked the closest player to you and launched the rubber ball so that it hit him on the fly. If you missed you got "asses up." This meant that you stood up against the wall bent over with your hands on your knees while every player threw two fastballs each at your butt. With 12 to 15 players each having two opportunities to hit you, you would often leave the game with welts all over your body. And God forbid you peaked through your legs as you bent over. Unfortunately, many a black eye was rung up by a well-placed eighty plus mile an hour from my neighbors Johnny Corrallo, Joe Palumbo and Tony Puma.

I loved to play roller hockey, but they didn't have a roller hockey team at school, so my Saturdays were spent either playing roller hockey in the park or playing stickball, softball or touch football in the school yard. But mostly roller hockey was my thing. Boro Park had a real roller hockey rink in it which was the most amazing thing in the universe to me. It worked out great that I ended up being a firefighter in that same area for almost 10 years!

Of course I graduated from High School. I just didn't hang out there any longer than I absolutely had to. I went to school and, just like I did in my early school years, I did whatever I had to do to get by. I didn't like to study. I wasn't really interested in anything. I never really understood how Algebra or Geometry or other subjects were going to help me so I put it all out of my mind. Believe it or not I did like history. I actually went to summer school and got a 99 in history because I was very interested in the subject matter and I applied myself. The class was taught by a young, creative, caring and hip guy who really knew how to get my attention. I was satisfied in knowing that I could succeed in school if I were interested in the right subjects.

As much as I enjoyed that particular class, I was still determined never to go back to summer school again. I had to go so I went. Most of the teachers gave passing grades to the students who showed up. There were a lot of girls in summer school with PHD's. You know, "phenomenal hair do's". They can chew gum and twiddle their hair at the same time. It's true. Summer school was just a matter of showing up. And even I could do that much! I was relieved when I finally graduated from New Utrecht High school in 1973. This is the school whose image is famously depicted in the opening montage for the TV show "Welcome Back Carter."

After high school I considered joining the Navy but I was quickly talked out of it by my dad. The Vietnam War was still going on in 1973 with no real indication of ending anytime soon. My dad said that he fought the war to end all wars and no son of his was going to war-end of discussion. The economy wasn't very good back then and the city was in the process of firing cops and firefighters, so I didn't look for employment in that direction. I was blessed and got a full-time job elsewhere. My high school job was working for a florist, so once I graduated I simply took more hours as they became available. I delivered flowers and learned how to make flower arrangements, but I wasn't really good at it. I was better at preparing the flowers and cutting them. Emeile was a phenomenally gifted florist and he was very successful.

I, on the other hand, didn't have the artistic touch. I tried, but God didn't bless me with that talent. My claim to fame was borrowing some of the flowers from the over the top *avalunedon* floral arrangements which was meant for dead people; and giving them to the most beautiful girls Bensonhurst had to offer, as well as their grandmothers. Grandmothers always liked me. I remember smoking pot in the van on a far delivery to Long Island with all these funeral arrangements. I stopped to pick up my friends because it was a long trip for a single delivery and I thought some company would be great. It wasn't until later that I learned that driving out to Long Island for a delivery and picking up my friends were two things that I should not have done and would not ever do again.

I was driving erratically after we stopped for burgers to make up some lost time. Some of my more rowdy friends were horsing around in the back of the van on the ride there. So the flowers kind of got like all mushed and mixed up. So when I stood in the parking lot of this funeral home in Long Island and I open up the doors I saw that the entire arrangement fell out of their designs in the Styrofoam holders.

Now some of these were these big crosses and hearts with doves on them and most of it fell out into the parking lot or was mushed. So here I am in the parking lot and one of my friends asks what I was going to do with them. I smirked and told him that I was a bona fide professional florist and I started snapping, breaking and sticking the pieces back in the Styrofoam centerpiece with breakneck speed. I needed to get in there quickly before anyone could figure out what was going on.

I ran the arrangements into the funeral home and went back to the shop hoping that no one would have noticed how wrecked the arrangements were or how stoned I was. Emile generally wore a shirt and tie. He reminded me of Floyd, the barber on the "Andy Griffin" show. When I got back to the shop I saw him wave me into the shop.

"They called," he announced.

As soon as I heard these words I just knew that I was going to be fired. I just did not know how much drama there would be in the process.

"Yeah, they called and they said that they were the most beautiful arrangements they've ever seen."

I guess they must have looked pretty good. Or at least they looked good enough for me to keep my job.

Since my days as a faux florist, I went on to have a variety of valuable life experiences. I stumbled through a few odds and ends jobs in Brooklyn before hopping on a plane to traverse the country and end up as a traveling ad salesman in Los Angeles around the age of 22. While in the city of Hollywood hopefuls I jumped head first into the dating game. It was not long before I lost miserably in the dating game and decided to return to Brooklyn where I could at least enjoy my mom's Italian home cooking with no strings attached. By the time I was 26 I was a NYC Sanitation Engineer. Like my dad, I had become a city worker. And finally, just before my 29th birthday, which is only one year away from the cut off age to become a firefighter, I went to *Proby School* to become a firefighter.

There were a lot of wrong turns taken at the right time that led me here. I can't say that I was that kid back in school who collected firefighter memorabilia and dreamed about putting out fires. Remember, I was the kid who did just enough to pass-just enough to get by. I wasn't motivated by much of anything back then other than sports.

Looking back I'm still not sure what made me decide to jump through all those hoops to be a firefighter. At that time, firefighters were only being hired once every 3-4 years and there were about 68,000 test takers who were competing to take one of the 2,500-3,000 spots in *Proby School*. At best this meant that about 1 out of every 25 test takers was going to make it. So it was not about "passing" the test, it was about out scoring at least 65,000 other people. Keep in mind that many of these applicants were the sons and grandsons of firefighters, lieutenants, chiefs and captains-so they definitely had a lot more inside information than the rest of us.

I had to take an 8-10 week course taught by firefighters and pass both a written and physical test before even being allowed to attend the *Proby School* at *The Rock* where I would have the opportunity to learn to be a firefighter. I actually took the test two times. It's not that I didn't plan for it. I did take the courses and I was good at the physical part, but it turns out that if you take someone who was never good at taking tests in school and then send him out to party in bars the night before a test, he doesn't stand a chance. Who knew? What helped me out was that I did great on the physical part of the test because of all the walking and heavy lifting on my sanitation job. I would purposely run through my routes to build strength and endurance with no shift relief changes. My daily co-partners loved working with me because all they had to do was drive. I would lift some seven plus tons of refuse by my lonesome and they were just fine with it. My weekend warrior love of hockey and other sports, sometimes pushing two-a-days in the gym, helped me stay in shape as well. It helped improve my score but not enough to make the cut. I was number 6,108 on the list.

The test was completely revised by the second time I took the test because the physical was modified to allow women the chance to join. This time my combined rating for both the written was a near perfect 99 and over 100 on the physical (I completed the course with 17 seconds to spare and the time was added to my final score as bonus points). I earned a list number of 305 without the benefit of the five bonus points that were offered to veterans.

The irony, which is the story of my life, is that I was hired off of the 6,108 score in the next to last class before the city officially killed the list. And after 12 more weeks of fire school at *The Rock* where I learned tactical firefighting, Fire Science, how to master Engine stretches, hook ups, hydrants, stand pipes, and Truck work, ladders, size-up, forcible entry, roof rope rescues and single slide emergency evacuation, auto extrications, basic EMT training and how to be a loyal pawn who takes orders in a quasi-military organization, I finally became a full-fledged firefighter in 1984.

The day I became a firefighter, or a *proby* in a firehouse, I knew that I was signing on for a career as someone who runs into the fiery nightmares that everyone else tries so desperately to escape. I knew that I was going to be exposed to tragic accidents. I even knew that there would be times when I wouldn't always know what to do right away. But I never knew there would be a day when I would be part of the efforts to restore a city that literally crumbled all around us. I never knew that I would lose so many of the firefighters who were my mentors and friends all at the same time. And I never knew that the events that tried to destroy the history of my country would also so permanently alter my future as a firefighter.

By September 11, 2001 I had 17 years of service dedicated to the FDNY and plans for achieving at least another 20 years. It's not unusual for a fireman to stay on for century long careers. Most of the chiefs serve for at least 20 years before they even take that position and then go on to serve for many more years. That was an option that I was interested in exploring until the absurd happened and started one of the most devastating times in my life as an adult.

9/11 was a disaster for all the brothers of the New York City Fire Department. We all had to deal with it in our own unique way. The trouble was that no one really knew how to deal with the trauma, grief, loss, and never-ending pain. Emotions ran the gamut of being silent as a mouse in the corner of the church to becoming a raging violent maniac in a moment's notice. The shift between the emotions could happen in any place at any time and in the company of anyone. The badly beaten remnant of what was known throughout the land as "The Bravest" was a tragic group of remaining lost, yet living, souls. The entire New York City Fire Department was in such a sad state of affairs. It's a miracle that they kept on functioning as a cohesive unit protecting the city they loved.

No division or battalion of therapists and psychiatrists had ever prepared for the most poignant assignments of working with fire fighters and police officers. We are trained to work under a well-defined code of regulations within a defined community. And although we committed to serve the public, there is nothing in our culture about being completely open and trusting of someone outside of the fire fighter brotherhood or our own biological families. Opening up to the people who help you escape from burning buildings or the ones who take care of you when you are sick is one thing, but opening up to someone who works in an office that is most often decorated with three or more college degrees is not a normal occurrence for us. It takes a special person with a lot of patience to earn the trust of salty fire fighters, get them to talk about what is tearing them up after working at Ground Zero, and then have them implement your ideas on how they can move forward. Besides, why would someone who has made an entire career out of going into life threatening disaster areas trust someone who spends most of their career in air conditioned offices? That is a tough sell, and not all of the mental health professionals were up to the challenge.

Some of the baptized-by-fire professionals retreated to find another profession. I have personally witnessed this and felt so sorry for them that I wished I had never stepped into their office to seek professional help. We were all broken toys. Forget all the professionals who tried to mend us. Even with all the degrees on their office walls that vaguely described what they were qualified to perform, this task was impossible for them to achieve. Although they faithfully and repeatedly tried their hardest time and again, this was a matter only the Lord Almighty could handle. I now know the meaning of mental paralysis. It is severe depression and loneliness that no one can cure.

September 11, 2001 was only the appetizer for my depression. It really set in weeks later when the series of funerals started. My very dear friend James "Jimmy" Giberson was 43 years old and had just celebrated his 20 years of service to the fire department only six days before his death at the World Trade Center on September 11, 2001. He was with Ladder 35. He was last seen entering the second tower about ten minutes before it collapsed. Jimmy was the kind of man who lived for his wife and three daughters. He would even skip out on fishing and other events with his friends just to spend the day with his daughters. He was just the kind of guy that you cannot help but to respect, and I was honored to have had him as my friend.

Jimmy's Memorial Service was on Friday, October 5th, 2001. By this date there were many funerals and memorial services simultaneously going on all over the city, especially on Staten Island, who lost the most firefighters on 9/11. I wanted to arrive early enough to enter the church-even if it meant that I had to stand near the back wall of the church. So I woke up at 6 am so that I could get out of Manhattan and into Staten Island on time for the 1 pm memorial. This was not the first service I had attended since September 11th, so I had an idea of what to expect.

All of the services and memorials were so overcrowded. It seemed as if you were in a subway car during rush hour. The church crowds overflowed into the church vestibule and down the steps. Firefighters from all over would come to pay their respects and they lined the walkways and roadways leading up to the church. Sometimes the line would stretch a quarter-mile in each direction. Each one of us wanted to be there to pay tribute to our fallen brother.

The horrific traffic on the way to the funeral gave me plenty of time to admire and duly note the beautiful clear weather outside. It was almost as clear as it was on the morning of September 11th. Although I thought my 6 am wake up time was early enough to secure a spot along the back wall of Christ Lutheran Church so I could pay my respects to my dear friend Jimmy Giberson and his family, the traffic made it clear to me that I still did not leave early enough. I had never attended this particular church before and this was well before it became popular to own a GPS that can conveniently re-route your journey when you run into traffic, so the only way I could get there was to follow my handwritten directions-even if it did require me to stay in traffic. I can't even describe the relief I felt as I saw the church steeple ahead as I approached a residential area where the traffic was starting to become even denser than before.

As soon as I saw the church steeple, I stopped looking down at my written directions and simply started following the traffic that seemed to be heading in that direction. Soon I approached the New York Police Departments traffic detail assigned to the funeral. They did a great job of leading us to parking lots and spots near the church. The church's parking lot was well over filled with cars parked on the grass and in other impromptu parking spaces that would usually be illegal. The lots were usually reserved for family and friends, but many of them never made it into that lot because of the sheer volume of cars carrying all the people who were in attendance at the funeral. I ended up parking about five or six blocks away from the church.

I lost my bearings while walking on the way back up to the church and decided to follow the masses of firefighters lining up in front of the church in both directions on the street. In most cases, it would have been a much longer line outside, but there were so many funerals and memorials that morning that each of us would have to choose which one to attend and we couldn't all show up in full force to all of them. Still, firefighters lined up in their Class A uniforms with polished shoes, white gloves and tears in their eyes.

I was mustered in rank-and-file without knowing who was on my right or my left. A fresh flow of tears filled my eyes as I stood at attention and saluted the battalion chief's car and the caisson, or an Engine that has been cleaned and had its hoses removed to make room for the casket and the attending pall bearers. You can always tell the difference between an active fire truck and one for a funeral because in a funeral the caisson truck is draped with a black mourning cloth. It is used specifically for firemen who gave their lives in the line of duty. The FDNY Pipes and Drums used their Scottish bagpipes and drums to play that same death march song that I've heard too many times before. I thought to myself that I never want to hear that march played again, ever. But deep down I knew all too well that it was going to be played several more times. In fact, the Emerald Society Pipes and Drums would play that same song at about 343 funerals in the two years following the fall of the twin towers.

Once the ever slowly approaching rig was just in front of me, I glanced through my tear filled eyes and saw "Engine 201." I peered again to see if I had misread the number, but the same words, "Engine 201" were still there. Jimmy should have been in a 35 Truck. Even if Ladder 35 had to use an Engine instead of a Ladder, the Engine his company shared a firehouse with was Engine 40, not Engine 201. I was at the wrong funeral. That was not my dear friend Jimmy Giberson in the Engine just in front of me. How could I have attended the wrong funeral?

I had just about lost it and started to collapse in a blurred, exhausted, dizzy and confused state when the two quick thinking brothers at either side of me quickly caught me and held me upright. I managed to regain my balance long enough to allow the procession to pass by and continue on to the church. I was just so shaken by the mistake I had made. I couldn't wrap my head around it.

Then I suddenly realized that I wasn't at the wrong funeral. There was no such thing as a wrong funeral because they all were the wrong funerals. Not one of those funerals had to happen if it weren't for the consuming hatred of complete strangers who decided to take innocent lives just to make a statement. I could feel myself slowly unraveling and becoming undone. The only way I knew how to pull myself together was to take action. Before anyone could even ask me if I was ok I bolted back to my car. I decided that I could still go and find the right church in time to see my friend Jimmy off. This was my new mission. It was simple enough. But once I made it back to my car I was shaking so badly that I couldn't put the key in the ignition to drive. Missing Jimmy Giberson's funeral will haunt me the rest of my life and it is already in the rotation of my weird and ugly reoccurring nightmares.

CHAPTER EIGHT

The Living Nightmare

As powerful and vivid my nightmares are about missing my friend's funeral, they still pale in comparison with the living nightmare that greeted me once I made it back to Manhattan after leaving the Engine 201 funeral. When I came back to the hotel Charlie was standing outside with our bags and demanding that we go to the doctor.

"What are you doing?" I asked.

I really wanted to take a shower, but he told me we couldn't go in there.

"What do you mean we can't go in there?"

I knew the room was paid for, so I didn't understand what he was going on about.

"No, no, no, we gotta leave. You gotta take me to the doctor. I gotta go to the doctor!"

Charlie was ashy and gray as he stood there trembling.

"You didn't go to that firehouse did you?" I asked although I was certain that I already knew the answer.

"Yeah!" He said.

"Well, let's go to the firehouse," I replied. If I couldn't shower in the hotel then I knew my old firehouse "The Pride of Midtown" Engine 54 Ladder 4, would let me shower there.

"No, don't go in the firehouse. Don't go in the firehouse!"

"Charlie, what are you talking about?"

"No, there's a problem, you gotta take me to my cardiologist. I gotta go to the doctor. I called him. You gotta take me to the doctor in Staten Island."

Nothing he was saying at the moment made sense to me, but the moment he said that he needed to see his cardiologist I decided not going to argue. Just a year prior my brother had open-heart surgery. The surgery lasted fifteen hours, and they built a defibulator into his chest. He's not a well man and I was not going to let anything happen to him on my watch. But I did make him tell me what had happened while I drove him to see his doctor.

We had come into the city together to participate in a fundraiser for the survivors and family members of those who lost their lives on September 11th. Although he is always eccentrically nutty, he was a retired NYC sanitation worker who never lost his love for his city. He was eager to help, just like everyone else. We had bought about a dozen hats at the fundraiser to give away to firemen. We decided to spend the night in the hotel because I wanted to be back in the city the next day.

Before I had left to attend the funeral, I specifically told him that after he wakes he should go to a specific diner on Broadway that I know serves a very inexpensive breakfast. I made perfectly clear, in no uncertain terms, that he should stay away from the firehouse where he and I had been volunteering for a few days. After the loss of 15 of their firemen, I knew that the house would be inundated with family and friends holding vigil and distraught firemen doing their best to keep doing their jobs. He acknowledged by repeating what I had told him before he rolled over and went back to sleep. When he got up later and left for breakfast he took the cell phone and my fireman shirt with my name on the back that I left for him. But he decided to leave my advice behind.

Outside of the firehouses were these makeshift memorials where people could pin up cards, candles, and flowers for the men who were lost. My old company, "Pride of Mid-Town" had lost 15 guys, probably the most ever of all the houses. In the meantime, they were still operating, so there were all kinds of emotions going on. My brother started helping the people coming by. They would hand him money, cards and even hand written notes of gratitude. He would pin the cards and notes up, and put the money in his pocket. He wasn't thinking to put it in the envelope and bring it inside. There was too much going on.

When some of the guys came back, one watched Charley slide the money into his pocket, and his emotions went crazy. He's the type of guy, when you ask him to go from A to B, goes from A to Z. Like I said, he's eccentrically nutty.

The guys put my brother in this house watch, and started accusing him of stealing.

"You're stealing money! What are you doing? You're stealing from the widows and orphans! Empty your pockets. Whose money is this?"

Charlie tried to explain the story, but some of the guys were trying to hit him and rip his head off while others were stepping up for his defense. They didn't know whether to call the cops or throw him out. Eventually, they just threw him out.

After he told me what had happened, all I could say was, "didn't I tell you *not* to go to the firehouse? I don't work there, you got my shirt on, guys are all emotional and things are going on. I worked there, but I don't work there anymore and you can't just do things like that. Like, maybe if you have a folder and you're putting it in the folder. But you shouldn't even be taking any money! I mean, just take the cards. I told you not to be there, there's too much going on. There were widows crying on the freakin' door step...I know you're trying to be helpful, everyone knows you're trying to be helpful, but look what happened!"

By the time we got to the doctor he was a mess. After they did all they could do for him there at the hospital he was ordered to go home and rest.

When I went back to my firehouse, they were waiting for me at the door. The anger in their eyes was enough to let me know that they wanted to kill me. They didn't even need to say a word to let me know how they felt, but they did anyway.

"We've got phone calls from downtown, uptown, every firehouse in the city. Every chief is calling and you're a thief," they said. "What are you doing? Why the fuck did you do it?"

They wouldn't let me speak or utter a response. If I stayed any longer they would have hung me in the basement, pretended that they found me a week later and called it a suicide.

"No, get the fuck out of here. You're on vacation. Don't go near a fucking firehouse. Don't go near anything. Don't go near Ground Zero."

My current firehouse captain was called up at home while he was on vacation and he didn't want to hear anything. He didn't really know me that well so his response was a little less than encouraging. He's the one who called me up,

"You stay away," he ordered.

"Yeah, but let me explain..."

"I don't want to hear shit from you! You're a fucking cancer. Get away! Just don't even go near a firehouse."

I was being ostracized. Everyone I knew was in this place and now I was being cut off from them. First, I missed my friend's funeral and now I was being cut off from the rest of the firemen I knew. I was already mentally and physically exhausted from weeks of alternating between working at Ground Zero and then attending funerals for fallen fire fighters. But now I was mortified. I was hurt. My brothers thought that I was a thief and a robber of widows and orphans. I was stunned and could barely find the words to speak.

"Don't call anybody, don't see anybody," they said. "You'll be notified by the IG's office. There will be a full investigation by the police department. Just go home or do us a favor and kill yourself."

There was no way that this was really happening to me. Neither me nor Charlie would ever do anything as crazy as what I was now accused of. The only thing crazy that Charlie would do was with cars. Charlie could do things with vehicles that nobody thought was possible. But instead of driving for NASCAR, he ended up getting a city job, like my father wanted for all of us, as a driver for the sanitation department. I watched my brother take a garbage truck and drive between the columns and the parked cars on a two-way street without hitting a single car or column. He has never lost his touch and can drive anything. He got married when he was 23 or 24 to a woman about 8 years his junior. His bride's uncle was an electrician and got Charlie into the business for a while. Then

Charlie left and became a sanitation worker, like his father-in-law, while the uncle when on to make millions with his business as an electrician.

In fact, none of my brothers would ever consider stealing from widows and orphans. We simply weren't raised that way. That wasn't the kind of stuff we were made out of. I just knew that Charlie didn't come all the way to Manhattan to attend a fundraiser with me on one day just so that he could steal money the next day. Besides, Charlie and I were the oldest of five siblings and not one of us lived a life as anything but public servants.

My younger brother Richie was more of a quiet kid. He was about a year-and-a-half to two years younger than me. I remember him carrying around a Huckleberry Hound stuffed animal. When he was five years old he used to wear shorts with button-down shirts and a bow tie while he carried a stuffed Huckleberry Hound around. I don't know why he wanted the bow tie. All I know is that my mother would have to bow tie him when we went to church or when we went to Grandma's house. He just liked the bow tie. For a couple of years that was how he liked to get dressed. My mother still has pictures of him wearing these bow ties.

Richie stayed in college until he took the summer job of being a postman and then never went back to college. He's still a postman today in New Jersey-not a city employee like our father wanted but dad wasn't disappointed that he became a federal employee. He's been a postman about 36 years. He always had a great route. People have given him their old cars. He's just that kind of guy. They make him lunch. They love him. He's the best. He always took care of people. "I'll take care of that. I'll straighten it out. I'll replace your light bulb or the batteries in your smoke detector." Whatever little trivial thing he could do for somebody that had no family, whatever, but that was what he did. When you hand deliver the checks every month when he did the buildings on Ocean Parkway in Brooklyn. He had a great route. He also had a good Christmas route. The people loved him. He didn't want to transfer to Jersey when he moved there, but now his route is in the senior development neighborhood and they love him just the same.

And what's not to love? He's great and he has a side business where he washes, repairs and installs window screens. He hired his two sons Chris and Matt to help him with the bull work and hired his daughter Jessica for moral support and to share time and stories with the lovely clients. Almost all of the proceeds go into his kid's pockets. He takes $100 for the supplies, a little bit of gas money and $50 for himself, the rest of it he gives to his kids.

He married the girl up the street from our childhood home, put his kids through college, and then got divorced. He still manages to be friends with his ex-wife. He's the quintessential best father in the world. He takes care of their cars, he does all that stuff for them that teenagers neglect to do or put aside. He's a good guy. He's a really good guy. He doesn't chase women. He loves the Green Bay Packers, the Baltimore Orioles, and the Boston Bruins (go figure) and fantasy sports but he is really all about anything and everything that has to do with his kids. That's all he does. He chases his kids to this day, and they're college graduates, His two boys Christopher and Matthew should be very proud of their dad for the sacrifices he has made on their behalf. His only daughter, Jessica, got a great job in the medical field after finishing school. All he said to her was, "make sure you stay on top of this and make sure you get that done," and he paid for everything. He is going to get married again in late September 2013 to a wonderful gal who happened to be his first love. It was his Kismet, his destiny. Richie's a great guy and it's time for him to share and enjoy a wonderful life with his new loving bride Linda and his new ten year old twins, the lovely Jessica and Corrine.

Craig went to the Marines and came back a different guy. He was a real passive guy when he left but he came back with the mind of a killer. He served in Iraq and in Kuwait for a total of a year following the September 11th attacks. As soon as he got out he got a job as a bartender with a catering hall where he met his wife. They got married in one of the top catering and special event venues in New York called Russo's On the Bay in Howard Beach. They worked there for a couple of years when it first opened and the owner wanted them to get married there and gave them a great deal. He wore his Marine dress blues and had several of his fellow Marines there with him, and she made an entrance up through the floor of the hall. It was amazing!

They had children, a boy and girl. And just like Richie, he made sure that his kids got everything they wanted and everything he thought they should want. Unfortunately, he also ended up divorced like Richie. His divorce was for a very different reason however. One day while Craig was in line at the airport with his wife, he told her how he was going to turn around and snap the neck of one of the guys behind them in line and then grab the second guy's leg and then cut his throat. She was so afraid of him that she got divorced. He never put a hand on her. He never assaulted her. But she just didn't feel safe around him anymore.

He went to see doctors and they diagnosed him with Post Traumatic Stress Disorder (PTSD). He was really quiet about it and none of us knew anything about it until this happened. Besides, by the time he came back I was already married and was starting a family with my own wife, so I wasn't overly involved with his personal affairs. He was always a good man, but the war changed him.

Even our younger brother Greg became a sanitation worker- another public servant.

By the end of the investigation they realized that it was unfounded. I was exonerated and indemnified by the city and all powers that be by being allowed to keep my job. Unfortunately, it didn't matter one iota that the investigation found me innocent because by the time the report was released the story had spread through the whole NYC fire department. Everyone thought of me as a scumbag thief. You would have thought that I had robbed three banks and murdered six people and ran over mother Teresa during the getaway. It didn't matter what the investigation uncovered or what I said. When I walked down the street and firefighters recognized me they would spit on me and call me a scumbag. No one wanted to talk to me.

"Don't even come near me. I don't even want to see you."

I was actually starting to get emotional because these were not just complete strangers who were upset with me. These were my friends who didn't even want to talk with me.

I had done some crazy things in my years as a firefighter, but none of them had ever elicited this kind of response. I remember getting a phone call at 9:00 in the morning after a long night of drinking and partying. As the phone rang I was scrambling around, I almost fell off the bed, rolling around to get the phone, "This is Captain Grasso. Why aren't you at work today?" I had been sleeping so rubbed my eyes and thought it was a prank.

"Are you shitting me? I'm off today, I'm not working today."

"No, Ron, I'm not shitting you!"

And all of a sudden I went from zero to 100. I was supposed to be at work already so all I could say was, "I'll be right there!" I don't think he even had time to tell me, "Take your time." Because he was that kind of guy that when he really knows you're coming, and if you're right, he'll kind of leave space in the book open for you. But he would never tell me that because I was a *proby*! I just knew that I needed to get from Brooklyn to mid-town Manhattan fast!

He'd write it in red when you'd get there, because everything's to the minute. It's all documented exactly to the minute. Firefighter Parker, RFD (ready for duty) at 7:59, or Firefighter Smith, RFD, 8:01. If someone doesn't show up you always leave a space in the book for their name and then talk to the officer or call the guy up before you call anybody, but I didn't get a phone call from any of these jerks because they probably didn't even know who I was.

I guess they knew I was supposed to come in because there was there was someone from the previous shift waiting for me to come in and relieve them. When I showed up that person's name would be crossed off the list and my name would be put in their place. Since there was someone waiting on a replacement, they had to know that I was missing.

At the time, I had a brand new souped-up 1983 Pontiac Trans Am Indy Pace Car that my girlfriend got from California. I drove through the Brooklyn Battery Tunnel when they were changing the lights from green to yellow to red, you know they're going to switch the sides, and there had been a little bit of traffic going in the tunnel. I drove through the Tunnel the wrong way out. I watched it go from green to red. That means they're going to open up the other side for people to drive in. But I did it in the same tunnel, so I was able to cross over if need be. I didn't choose to go in a different tunnel, because then if you get stuck you're screwed, you're done. But I think I made it to Ladder 4 Manhattan in about 14 minutes that day. When I arrived the captain raised his eyebrows and gave me a look of surprise that seemed to ask,

"You're here? Didn't I tell you to take your time?"

It was one of those days. And although it is unheard of for an FDNY firefighter to sleep through his shift, it was shaken off and merely dismissed; although I did polish a lot of brass that week. There was no drama behind it.

The other unflattering way I ran into the captain was when I drove my motorcycle into Manhattan from Brooklyn. I remember trying to figure out the best way to go. With the motorcycle you can squeeze through traffic so you can save time. I was between 3rd and Lexington heading west on 42nd St. I was in the right lane and was preparing to make a right turn. There was a red light, but that wouldn't stop me from making my turn. And there was a truck in front of me and a cabbie came up from the left side. He was coming all the way over with bad intentions. I watched the driver weave through the traffic, but he never looked at me. He didn't even notice me as he swerved at a high rate of speed into the turning lane where I was and pushed me out of the lane.

I got nudged into the high curb and pushed right on to the sidewalk where I just dropped my bike. He didn't hit me hard as he forcefully braked and knocked me over. I could feel the blood rushing into my face and throbbing as the self-righteous anger of a young man grew in me. I was going three miles an hour and I let every cuss word fly out of my mouth in every possible combination that I could think of.

I used to carry my spare helmet under my elbow, like an elbow pad. It was a shortie-helmet, so I would have my helmet on, and then carry the other one because I didn't have a place to put it. So I remember screaming at this guy, and the guy's looking at me with an expression that seemed to say, "I don't know." He didn't see anything and I was still upset about my bike being pushed to the ground and scratched. So I gave him a little shove with my spare helmet through the window to release him of his zombie stare.

The next thing I knew he grabbed me and then I grabbed him. We started pulling at each other through the cab window. When I heard the sirens of the quickly approaching cops I really got upset because I had to get to work and didn't have time for any of this crap. So I just jumped on the motorcycle and rode off towards my firehouse on 48th and 8th. I was about a half mile away on 42nd and I still had to deal with the traffic.

When I finally got to the firehouse I pulled into the little courtyard where you could put either one car, or guys used to put their bicycles, and in my case my motorcycle. It was the same courtyard where the senior firemen sent me out to check on the barbecue only to douse me with all that water. I put my bike in there and I went into the house. I was basically on time but I still had to go upstairs to do a quick-change. When I went back down the stairs I saw two detectives and I just knew they were looking for me.

One of them looked up at me and said, "you left the scene of an accident and you beat up this cab driver."

For the second time that morning I could feel my heart pounding and all of the blood rushing to my head, but I try to play it cool, "Yeah,

I had some kind of altercation with some asshole cab driver, you know?" My cool demeanor didn't make them change their minds, and they put me in their unmarked police car and they took me down to their precinct so I could tell these detectives what happened. I told them how the guy landed me and my bike down on the ground, but all I heard back was, "Yeah, but he's all beat up." Oh my God! Well, somebody had to win! I was so annoyed by the entire situation and I was not afraid of showing it. I finally look at one of the cops and try to level with him, "Hey, I've got to work, what are you doing? Someone who just worked a 15 hour shift is working overtime to cover my assignment until I get back."

Before I knew it, the rig from my firehouse was outside the police station to pick me up and the captain was in there. He walked in and layed into the first person he sees, "Hey listen, I followed the cop car, what are you jerks doing?"

They start explaining the situation to my captain but he doesn't let up, "Is this guy in the hospital?"

I didn't put him in the hospital. I had only roughed him up a bit. By the end of the conversation we learned that there was a lady in the back of the cab and she had no clue about how the cab driver had knocked me over. She thought I just attacked this guy through the window for no reason, so she called the cops.

When Captain Grasso heard that the cab driver wanted to press charges he started asking more questions. He found out from the detectives that the cab driver had a driving record that unfolded as long as Bullwinkle's calling card and that the cab driver had a suspended driver's license. This made it easier for them to believe that he had run me off the road. My captain reassured them that if they didn't lynch me at high noon he would discipline me himself. No one cared about the damage to my bike because I didn't have a scratch on me and the other guy looked a little worse for the wear and the detectives kept bringing up the fact that I had left the scene before they arrived.

You can imagine how they felt about it when I decided to simply walk out of the station so I could get back to work. Besides, I knew that I didn't murder the guy or do any serious, permanent damage. This was unnecessary drama that was keeping me from doing what I needed to do. Once I got outside I saw the rig and all I could do was sigh. After about 6 months as a *proby* firefighter, this was how I finally met the captain. When I got back to the firehouse a senior guy with about 30 years on the job walks up and looks down at me and says, "So we got a criminal working with us, huh?" I remember feeling a little nervous about how the firemen were going to take it, but next he said, "Get to work," and the other guys start clapping like it was a joke. Instead of ostracizing me for ending up in a police precinct, my captain defended me and everyone treated it like a joke instead of ostracizing me. However, he did keep his word to the police officers by making me do all of the house watch duty and spiffy up more of the truck's brass hardware.

But even I had to admit that this situation was different from the others. Now all of us were mentally and physically drained while we struggled each day to help rebuild a city that was destroyed by people we didn't know who attacked us for reasons none of us understood. At the time, there was a nameless and faceless villain out there who brought all of this on us. So when allegations arose about a theft by someone who could be identified, the distraught firefighters finally had a scapegoat villain they could punish. I never signed up to play that role, but I guess that someone had to sooner or later.

I was smart enough to vacate their presence. As the days passed and the anger didn't, I didn't know what to do. I had to reach out to somebody who would just listen to me and hear me out. I had few options. I didn't want to go upstairs with this although there was a chief there who knew me pretty well. He was pretty well respected downtown and he used to be my lieutenant in that Manhattan firehouse consisting of Engine 54, Ladder 4 and Battalion 9. He led me in some of the most rip roaring tenement fires, teaching me many a great skill as he operated flawlessly with jackrabbit speed and agility. Joe was a nice guy, a real good decent fair guy, real smart guy-a superbly gifted fireman and officer. He had the big office. I want to say he was in the top 20-25 of the chiefs in the NYC fire department. Reluctantly, and with my tail between my legs, I went downtown to see him.

"I gotta tell you what happened."

So I finally went downtown and told the whole story to the chief.

"Chief, I swear, this is exactly what happened."

"Well, I understand..." he said.

It turned out that he knew my current captain well.

"You know, I'll call your captain and see."

He actually called him right then and there but the captain didn't want to talk to him. Here was this chief who was respectfully calling a lower ranking captain and the captain's response was that he didn't want to hear it. He was on vacation and that was that. A real class act, NOT.

So the chief told me to go on home and that this thing would pass. Sshhh, it wasn't passing! So I went back to the firehouse, and these guys still wanted to kill me. I mean, the guys didn't want to talk to me. No charges were ever pressed against me since the investigation showed that I wasn't there and that he hadn't actually taken the money, but no one wanted to hear anything, it didn't matter. Eventually I decided that the best thing to do was just to volunteer for the details that no one else wanted so I could still work but be away from everyone else. Nobody wants to go to *The Pile*, so I'll go to *The Pile*. I'll take this detail, not a problem.

I took the detail and went right back in to Ground Zero. I worked through the end of Thanksgiving. I worked through Christmas. I worked through New Year's Eve and on New Year's Day I actually found a brother firefighter from Brooklyn's 201 Engine. The same company's funeral I had accidentally attended months before in lieu of my friend Jimmy's funeral.

I jumped into a hole, found a coat and started digging and digging and digging. He was upside down. So I laid backward because our bunker gear includes boots, pants, heavy duty suspenders and a coat that is all one unit so that it stays intact. I soon realized there was no helmet, there was no head. So I'm jumping into this hole and trying to get him. And it was really, really unbelievable. As I was digging him out I realized that I even knew the hero firefighter. He was Christopher Pickford of Engine Company 201, another Brooklyn brother. I was getting him out as carefully and as respectful as humanly possible. I wrapped him up in the flag and gently placed him in the Stokes basket. Just as we had for every other person recovered from the site, we stopped everything and shut the site down to carry our brother, Christopher Pickford, out of the bowels of that hell hole pit up to the top as all the brothers and workers silently lined up and saluted farewell to a true hero. I think that New Year's Day we found at total of six people. The closure was good for the grieving families.

That was one of my last details that I served in Brooklyn. The tension in the Staten Island firehouse got to be so bad that I ended up trying to transfer, but no one was doing me any favors by allowing me to transfer into their firehouse. I was stuck to rot there for the duration of my career.

To this day, many guys won't talk to me. They just don't even care. I don't know. And everybody else just went, "oh, we made a mistake. Ok." Honestly, I think of all the guys who really ostracized me there was one lieutenant who was a class act-he apologized to me, "I'm sorry."

"Thanks a lot. It means a lot to me."

Not that I thought that the whole company would, but they were a bunch of deadbeats that were controlled by a few bullies. I mean, to be honest, they worked on the very end of Staten Island and they didn't really want to put out any fires. They weren't that kind of gung ho company. There was a construction worker who owned a big business and he seemed to treat the fire department as his part time job. It was like where they came to go to sleep, I think. I don't know. And I never worked in a company like that. Not to put down Staten Island companies. Not at all since most of the men who work in the firehouses of Staten Island are brave and dedicated to their profession and do a fair amount of fire duty on the island's north shore and other over populated run-down neighborhoods. But this was certainly not the career I had in mind when I became a *proby* so many years ago.

It had become apparent that the time for retiring was on the horizon. I shunned the thought many times, but it inevitably it kept popping up in my head. I often asked myself if I was considering retirement on my own terms or on someone else's terms? Over the years I learned that passing the torch of the New York City Fire Department was recognized as being just as important as taking your first steps into *Proby School*. The perfect balance of learning, communicating and teaching were a delicate part of passing the torch.

This final phase has been realized by many as one of the most difficult, indelible and intricate decisions made in the career of a New York City firefighter. Some firefighters have that decision stolen from them due to injuries incurred on-the-job and forced out. Still others have made their last fateful steps precariously into a literal blaze of glory.

The last few months leading up to my May 12, 2004 retirement date were mostly spent alone in a quiet and tranquil bubble. The time passed by slowly, painfully slow. On my last day I finally emptied my locker barely looking or reminiscing about its contents as I had done in the past when moving my items to transfer from one house to another. In times past, I would always come across something that was forgotten. The rediscovery would bring a good chuckle and a smile to my face, but not this time. This was not a time for reminiscing because part of my reason for leaving was to forget.

Knowing that I was doing it for the very last time, I finished cleaning out my locker in record time. I packed my gear and quietly left. Hardly a goodbye was uttered by anyone. It was as if a ghost was leaving. I knew that I had accomplished all that I could have as a New York City firefighter, so a calm rewarding solace and peace embraced me as I left the quarters of Engine 164 and Ladder 84, the house known as "Close to the Edge."

The smile on their faces told me that Judy and my kids were happy with my new found freedom at home. I was also happy to be able to spend more time with them and I also wore a smile more often. However, mentally I was still a train wreck about being relieved of my duties as a fireman. It was beginning to destroy the man I was. I became more distraught, angry and confused. I began to question things that I couldn't go back and change.

My time was spent mostly at home alone becoming a recluse for the first time in my life. I avoided people at all costs. I wasn't comfortable around anyone other than my immediate family. I let a great deal of time pass and I let the distance between me and my friends grow as I continued to hardly speak to any of them. When we did speak I was uninterested, brief and curt over the phone. The days of getting together with friends for club hockey, golf and softball games became a distant memory. I simply had no interest feeling the way I did when I was still the man I knew and recognized-when I was still a loved and respected firefighter.

CHAPTER NINE

Creative Release

It was one of those bitter cold winter nights. Not much was happening in our battalion which was kind of unusual, considering the cold. So we should have known that it wouldn't be that way for long.

Teddy is a fearless firefighter on duty at one of our own battalion's firehouses on Manhattan's West Side-Engine 40 Ladder 35 on 66th St. and Amsterdam Avenue. Unbeknownst to the sleeping city, this fearless firefighter doubles as an off-duty recluse and drunk. And now that Jekyll was off-duty, he had transformed into Hyde for the sleepy evening. The rapidly approaching date of a divorce he didn't want inspired a steady pace of all-night binge drinking in an attempt to drown his sorrows. After failing to find a resolution at the bottom of several empty glasses, he left the bar to wander alone and dazed around the west side of the city.

Lost in his slurred thoughts about the divorce, he failed to notice the uneven sidewalk and he stumbled and fell into the glass window of the 24 hour doughnut shop. Fortunately, there was no damage to the glass. However, there happened to be two of New York City's finest sitting directly on the opposite side of the shop's glass window, and the startling crash prompted one officers to squeeze his jelly doughnut hard enough so that it squirted all over his uniform while the other officer spilled his hot coffee in his lap.

The coffee drenched officer immediately reached for the glass of ice water and doused his lap to relieve the excruciating pain from the piping hot liquid. Teddy watched the entire chain of events and instantly unleashed his signature laugh and howl. He laughed so uncontrollably that he emptied his bladder and his bowels onto the front and back of his own pants. But even this self-degrading display was not enough to appease the officers and allow him to escape their crosshairs.

The cop covered in jelly doughnut was Officer Muldoon. He was a hard-nosed, no-nonsense tough, jelly doughnut loving cop who demanded respect. And Teddy's unbridled laughter infuriated the officer and now he sought revenge. His partner had an interesting reputation of his own. The coffee drenched officer was notorious Bend-a-cop Sullivan who earned his nickname by repeatedly writing summonses to fellow off-duty police officers and their families. But on this night he was not after any other cops, he was after the man who caused his favorite evening coffee to end up scorching his lap.

Out the door they came as furious and ravenous as any human can possibly be. They were way passed angry. The steam coming out of their noses as they forcefully exhaled into the cold night air was so intense it appeared as if the fire of a jet engine was embedded within the exhaust of their breath. There was even a trail of steam radiating from Officer Sullivan's lap as he moved. And Muldoon's uniform resembled a cinematic depiction of a bloodstained shot down gunslinger in a Sam Peckinpah's Western that used jelly to imitate the blood. The intense look on their faces suggested that this was not a laughing matter. But Teddy and the two night shift working men in the doughnut shop still managed to appreciate the humor of the spectacle and could hardly contain themselves.

The officers reached Teddy in exactly the same place where they first laid eyes on him. He was now rolling and wallowing on the pavement still uncontrollably laughing.

"So you think you're funny. Do ya? I'll show you what's funny," said the giant sized Muldoon in his Irish brogue accent as he towered over Teddy.

Muldoon quickly grabbed Teddy by the collar and lifted him off the ground just in time for Sullivan to let loose with a quick punch to Teddy's gut. The blow triggered a fresh release of feces and urine that leaked through Teddy's trousers and embedded a fresh new smell into the already jelly-stained uniform Muldoon wore.

"What the hell are you doing?" Teddy chimed in. "It's me, Teddy, your brother-in-law!"

Muldoon quickly dropped Teddy back to the ground in a clump as he refocused his blood-red angry eyes long enough to recognize his kinfolk. Teddy leaned over onto his side and quickly dropped to sleep. He was completely oblivious of the mess he was in and the fact that he was laying outside on a sidewalk.

"He's a firefighter. We best drop him off at his firehouse where he will do no more harm. We'll let those crony old hosebags babysit him. It's only a few blocks from here."

They procured a body bag from the trunk of the squad car and carefully placed it in the back seat before loading Teddy into the cruiser to prevent further damage. Cleaning a uniform was one thing but having to clean the cloth bucket seats of the squad car they spent their entire shift in was another.

After hitting a series of potholes, Teddy momentarily awoke from his stupor to find that he was wrapped in the all familiar body bag and bouncing around in the back of a car.

"Let me out" he screamed from the top of his lungs.

Teddy knew Muldoon's Family had an extremely dark side and he thought he was going to be "deep sixed" in the Hudson River by the cop whose sister he married. He never spoke to anyone about the dark side of the Muldoon family. Not even to Father Mulligan at St. Patrick's Cathedral who he occasionally shared a pint or two with. Not even at Holy confession was this ever muttered. Although Teddy knew that his in-laws were active members of The Westies, the infamously crazy and deadly street gang feared by even the Italian mafia, he didn't find out until after he had already fallen in love and proposed. Once he found out it was not like he had many options. He couldn't break her heart and call of the engagement and expect to live through the end of the day. Teddy was stuck, or at least he was until the issue of divorce started coming up more and more in conversations with his wife.

Hell's Kitchen in Manhattan's West Side from the Midtown tunnel on the south side and up to Central Park was their domain. The Irish immigrant neighborhood gang isn't all that large in numbers considering the amount of crime, murder and havoc they wreak. Mostly void of formal education, street smarts is their forte. They all have master's degrees in robbery, kidnapping, arson, killing, dismembering, lying and cheating. And they all have a doctorate in drinking.

They are also great with their hands, knives, guns, as well as anything they can get their hands on becomes a precise and lethal weapon. They have been known to chop off their adversary's hands, store them in a freezer and use the fingerprints on guns and knives to cover their tracks. I'm sure if you Google psychopaths they're on top of the list. They could do you bodily harm, all accomplished without a blink of an eye with no remorse. What would appear to be a friendly conversation may turn deadly in a nanosecond. Sometimes you could become an adversary if they just didn't like your face.

You wouldn't want to be in any of the Westside local bars in Hell's Kitchen and even glance or make eye contact with any of them or else they might just kill you for fun. It all depended on their flippant mood. Upon entering any one of these watering holes, you would be eyeballed up-and-down within seconds. If you didn't pass the eyeball test and you were unfortunate enough not to have Spidey Senses or any inert ability to realize you're in the Devil's Lair, you may make the deadly mistake of taking an unwelcomed seat at the bar where they hold court. Physically kicking you out the door while they rifle through your pockets would be considered a blessing. The alternative might be separating your hands from your body to give them a new set of fingerprints.

Inspired by the mostly vacant and unused waterfront just a few blocks west of their location, Sullivan and Muldoon briefly discussed introducing the maligned and stinky Teddy to the Hudson. They had already wrapped him inside the body bag and it would not be difficult for each of them to grab and end of the bag and send him on his watery journey. Sullivan made a quick right turn and headed to the Westside piers.

All appeared quiet on the waterfront. There was not a soul in sight and even street lamps were broken and not watching over them. It was too bitter cold for the usual bums, vagrants and transsexual hookers to be out that brutal night. A couple of frozen dead wharf rats were all they found. I don't know how close they really came to deep sixing Teddy. They would have had to chop and break the ice in the Hudson just to get the body in the water. That was too much work and they didn't have the proper tools. Sullivan said they could've used their six-shooters, but they'd have to explain where the bullets went and it might make too much noise.

As Teddy heard the gist of the conversation between the two flatfoots he violently began to flail about as he tried to escape.

"You'll never get away with this!" Teddy slurred in defiance from the back seat.

Fortunately for Teddy, the consensus was to drop him off at his firehouse on Amsterdam and 66th Street and let them deal with the drunken mess that rightfully so belonged to them.

By the time the car finally came to a stop, Teddy's senses were awake enough to let him know that he was in a safe and very familiar setting. He was back at the quarters of Engine 40 Ladder 35-home of the "Cavemen". Sullivan hit a few of the trash cans that had been set out that evening as they pulled up to the apron of the firehouse. The action only seemed to disturb the one eyed firehouse cat affectionately known as Blinky. He was interrupted from his meal soirée of Chinese food, lasagna, pizza, chili tomato soup and borscht that was all freshly deposited a short time ago. But when house watchman O'Donavan heard the noise outside the firehouse at 4:15 in the morning he too prepared for action.

It was not unusual for victims of muggings or rape to arrive at the firehouse door for assistance. So in case he was to meet both the victim and the attacker, he armed himself with a baseball bat and opened the door to greet the source of the noise. As he stepped just outside the doorway, he saw Teddy in his distressed state with a big smile on his face. Muldoon and Sullivan were cursing Teddy on their way back to their cop car. Teddy clutched the side of a trash can with one hand to help him get back on his feet while the other hand clutched Muldoon's cigarettes he so deftly lifted from his oblivious brother-in-law when he bumped into Muldoon after he got out of the car.

Teddy stumbled past the bewildered O'Donavan who holstered the 44oz Louisville Slugger in its custom built rack on the side of the house watch wall. The house watchman shook his head as he retreated to his desk and tried to count how many times he had seen Teddy on such a familiar bender after a crazy night out. He sighed as he debated whether or not to report Teddy's condition to the firehouse officers in hopes that they might force him to go into rehab for his own good.

Teddy somehow managed to liberate his alcohol abused body from his fouled clothing as he managed to walk, crawl and pull himself up the steps to the firehouse recreation room. By the time he reached the couch he was only wearing his raccoon skin hat while he still clutched his newly acquired cigarettes. He decided to rest on the couch for a little while before heading off to the showers. He conveniently found the matches on the coffee table in front of him and lit up a cigarette just before he turned on the TV. He dosed off into a slumber only seconds after lighting the fateful butt.

Downstairs the banging was much fiercer than the sound he heard upon Teddy's arrival, so once again O'Donavan opened the door armed with the slugger. Two N.Y.C. sanitation workers were there to report a fire that was erupting out the window of an adjoining building on the 66th St. side of the block. But as Danny stepped outside to take a look, he noticed that it was not the other building that was on fire, it was his own firehouse that hosted the roaring flames.

O'Donavan quickly ran inside the firehouse and tapped three bells before he urgently, yet professionally, summoned both the Engine and the Truck companies over the house intercom. At the sound of the bells the brothers in the house quickly began to grab their gear to respond. But when he announced that the 1075 code for working fire was located in our own firehouse, some of the groggy brothers thought they'd misheard what O'Donavan said. Others were confused by not hearing the usual *bee-boop* sound from the tele-printer that always proceeded the ringing of the bells and the intercom announcement before a run. Still others said nothing even though they smelled smoke, thinking that it was a lingering smell from someone's gear from the last run.

O'Donavan repeated the announcement again and again while he managed to climb into his own gear. Thank God the Engine Captain was working that night as well as a senior lieutenant in the Truck. The Captain realized the severity of the problem and quickly asked O'Donavan if he had reported the fire to dispatch.

"I didn't think you would have wanted me to, Captain."

Engine 40 Captain sighed in relief that no one was notified and gave a slight nod that let O'Donavan know he had made the right decision. It's bad enough to have a fire in the firehouse without everyone else knowing about it. The Engine Company stretched the hose line up the interior steps of the firehouse towards the recreation room where the flames seemed to be coming from. The Engine's chauffeur left the lights and sirens off as he pulled the Engine a few feet out from the firehouse to line up with the fire hydrant that was in front of the firehouse and quickly hooked the hose up to the hydrant.

The Truck also pulled out of the firehouse without lights or sirens to make a right turn up 66th Street. The *OV* and *roof man* grabbed a 35 foot extension ladder and quickly made their way to the top of the building where they vented the roof by opening the bulkhead door to create a place for the fire to vent once the hose was turned on. They also quickly looked over all four sides of the roof before reporting over the radio to the lieutenant that the roof was open and there were no victims outside any of the perimeters of the building. 35 Truck's lieutenant and forcible entry team grabbed their hand tools and donned their masks before joining Engine 40, who was flanking out their line up the steps in preparation for battle with the flames.

They knew the layout of their own home all too well, and there were no doors to force open in search of flames or trapped victims. They just needed a thorough search for any firemen in distress because of the fire and a little venting for the flames and all should be well. The room was fully *involved* with fire by the time they reached it with the hose line. Engine 40's captain gave the order over the radio to "start water" and the Engine 40 chauffeur reported back a second later that it was on the way.

Engine 40 stretched inch and three-quarter line fast and steady in the aggressive interior attack of the fire. Ladder 35 *iron's man*, who carried tools to force open doors or remove any large obstacles obstructing a safe exit, gave a preliminary report to the Truck lieutenant that the initial search was negative, soon followed by the same response from the *can man* who always entered fires with a small fire extinguisher to knock down the fires on his way to finding any victims. The officer of 35 Truck also reported that there was no one in the sitting room and that there was a secondary search underway.

Engine 40's *nozzle man* and his backup who secured and maneuvered the rest of the hose line did a superb job in knocking down the fire in just a few minutes. Once the last of the flames was extinguished, the firemen started to wonder out loud how the fire started in the first place.

"Maybe it was electrical," one fireman offered.

It could have been electrical or overloaded circuits. Each of them wondered why no one knew the answer to what would become their dark and embarrassing firehouse secret as O'Donavan suddenly remembered Teddy's arrival shortly before the whole episode began. Where was that drunken fool? O'Donavan used his handi-talkie to report that Teddy was in the quarters and for everyone to look for him. He guessed that Teddy might know how this disaster began.

It turned out that Tri-pod, the three-legged firehouse dog, paid Teddy a friendly visit and cuddled with the drunk on the couch at the time Teddy lit his cigarette. He probably liked all the funky and unusual smells emitting from Teddy. When the couch erupted into flames it burned the poor pooch's good rear leg. Tri-pod bit the slumbering Teddy several times to wake him before they both retreated to the bathroom.

Now that he had finally made it into the bathroom, Teddy turned on the shower faucet only to fall asleep beneath the steady flow of the firehouse shower. He was totally unfazed by what was occurring all around him, and Tripod faithfully stayed by his side.

The Truck search team found Teddy in the shower a few minutes after O'Donavan's tip. Upon their less than silent arrival, Teddy awoke, saw the men in the full gear and asked his brother firefighters if the Captain had them drilling in the middle of the night. Although they did not yet know the full story, the lingering smell of urine, feces and alcohol told them what they needed to know. They left Teddy in the running shower while they tended to Tripod's burnt rear leg.

Miraculously, the city of 2 million Manhattanites remained unaware of the fiasco that had just taken place in one of their city firehouses in spite of the half dozen national TV Broadcasting offices, newspapers, and media centers within a few blocks from the firehouse in any one direction. Only the two N.Y.C. Sanitation workers who reported it to O'Donavan knew that there had been a fire that bitter night. Their discretion earned them a lifetime supply of fresh hot coffee, bagels and (don't tell Muldoon) jelly donuts any time they passed by the firehouse on their allotted break.

The following day, the 9th Battalion Chief showed up on his daily rounds. The Chief's car was parked on the apron of the firehouse as usual. His aide, Harris a salty 29 year veteran, strolled in with Chief Rooney, one of the most respected chiefs in the fire department. His time on the job eclipses Harris' by more than a decade. His invaluable knowledge has been utilized many times throughout his career.

Upon entering the *quarters* the *proby* sitting on house watch duty announced "Battalion 9 chief in quarters," which prompted an immediate lining up of all officers and members for roll call. Harris exchanged the inter-office mail bag with the *proby* on the watch as he turned and asked the senior man and Engine 40 chauffeur, Allen

Fineberg, if he had missed a job the previous night. Allen simply shrugged in response.

The chief dismissed the men after roll call and continued up the stairs to the firehouse office. Followed by the captain of 40 Engine and the lieutenant of 35 Truck, the chief stopped at the top of the stairs and then quickly turned around to descend back down the stairs. On his way down he growled, "I don't know how you jokers pulled it off, but I'm coming back for a full house inspection in a week and by then all of this would have been a mirage." He put his chief's hat on and entered the 9th battalion GMC suburban. Harris, his aide and driver, slowly pulled away from the firehouse. Not a word was uttered as they drove off.

"And that's my 'Teddy the Firebug' story that I've been writing," I proudly announced as I neatly stacked all of the papers containing the story to the side and looked up at my psychiatrist, Dr. Charles Carluccio, for a response.

I started seeing Dr. Carluccio at the recommendation of my friend and neighbor, Mike Kevlin. Mike was a neighbor of mine while I was still living in New Jersey. We were very, very close friends thanks to our kids and our friendly neighborhood. My son, Blaze, and his son, Michael, were in the same class together in school. So it wasn't long before Mike and I started to recognize each other at the boys' various sporting events, while walking the dog around the neighborhood, at the grocery store and just driving through the area.

An interesting note about Mike is that he had a lot of personal connections to the World Trade Center. He has an amazing story that's ironic.

17 years old, Mike became a United States Marine during Vietnam. It was probably around 1966 or 1967. He went overseas to Vietnam and he landed in the middle of the night.

"Corporal Kevlin," they tell him, "take this jeep with this canon on the back of it about 10-12 miles away by yourself at night with no lights on. Welcome to Vietnam, son!"

And he was definitely on the cusp of enemy territory when they leave this camp. It's not like he was on a highway. He was definitely in danger and he was by himself. He had an order and a jeep and that was that. He completed his task.

Mike was trained in the Marines-he had a passion for radios and he was a ham radio operator as a kid. He used to go to Radio Row quite often to buy all of these components and parts and ham radio antennas and enhancers and transistors. He would go by there all the time. There were a lot of stores in that area along the streets that had all these type of equipment that he could buy relatively cheap because it was all surplus military stuff from WWII and Korea.

Now, as a Marine, he just got there and had the latest training from the US Marine Corps to operate their radios for aerial bombardments, mortar placement, ships, guns, and also to communicate with the troops on the ground. If a convoy went out, Mike's jeep was in the middle of the convoy and protected to the utmost because it had top secret radio state-of-the-art technology. It wasn't just the standard day-to-day walkie talkie. He was the liaison to communicate commands and reports both to and from different battleships and ground troops. He knew how to operate all of it. That's why they made him Corporal and gave him his own jeep with his own name on it.

Mike will never fly in a plane though. If I told him that I'll send him a first class ticket to come visit me he would drive. On one of his deployments during Vietnam, he got on a small plane that crashed upon landing and split in half. He found himself tumbling out of the back of the plane. He wasn't killed, but he will never go on a plane again. In the military, he had to get on a plane a couple times after that so he could get back home, but he'll never get in a plane again. It's another ironic thing that he survived this plane crash and survived the plane crashes later on September 11th that killed almost 3,000 people.

Both his father and his grandfather were iron workers who built bridges, tunnels and buildings, so when he came out of Vietnam he became an iron worker. It was the nepotism thing. He was Irish and almost all the kids in his neighborhood were iron workers. He worked on buildings in downtown Manhattan and he watched the World Trade Center go up while he was on his work site. And he definitely did some work on the World Trade Center during periods when they needed extra guys to finish the job. He wasn't assigned to it at the time, but he did end up doing some iron work on the World Trade Center.

Then he became a Port Authority cop and the next thing you know he worked inside the building that he helped build as a Port Authority sergeant.

His story is pretty amazing how it keeps tying back to that area. First, when it was Radio Row. Then he was part of the crew that helped to build the World Trade Center. And finally he was a Port Authority sergeant who would be in that building every single day before he went back to New Jersey to sign out. It's also ironic that he was deathly afraid of planes after the crash that he survived, and then he survived the crash that destroyed the building and the area where he hung out as a child, the exact building that he helped build, and the building where he worked. If he had stayed on that job another eight or nine months he would have been killed by that plane although he vowed never to get into one again since Vietnam.

He knew many of the Port Authority police officers that were killed there, so in a lot of ways he probably understood what I was going through a little better than any of my other non-firefighter friends. Because he lived so close to me, I'm sure that he noticed that I was often down in the dumps and I just wasn't being the fun-loving guy that I normally was. I don't know if he ever noticed how I stopped doing things around the house like taking the garbage pails out. I don't know if he noticed that I would walk and talk to myself around the cul-de-sac that I lived in. Maybe he caught a glimpse of me stumbling or bumbling after I had been drinking. Then again, it could have just been his cop instincts that told him I needed someone to talk to me.

Whatever the reason, he did a little asking around and got me the contact information for Dr. Collucio.

"This is the guy that guys use when they have a problem. He's great and he's a local."

At first, I was forced to see the psychiatrist. Everyone else wanted me to see him, but I was not on that ship. I was disenchanted and disconnected from nearly everyone around me. I wasn't accepting any of the group help or any of the psychologist recommendations offered by the firefighter community or anyone else who was trying to reach out to those who had worked at Ground Zero. Deep down I knew that I really needed help. I knew that I couldn't just John Wayne it any more. My life was unraveling day by day. I drank a little more than I normally did, which wasn't all that often at first. Then over time I slowly began to empty more bottles. Every day I became more sluggish and useless.

I was very depressed. My sleep was interrupted by ever reoccurring nightmares that were very scary and intense to say the least, so I started taking naps during the day to try and compensate for the lack of sleep. I didn't exercise as much as I used to and I started gaining weight. I stopped caring about my appearance and it was starting to show in various ways. I quickly became a cranky and difficult old man and I was still in my late 40's.

Dr. Charles Carluccio was the key that helped me unlock and release my fears. We began to battle and defeat my ever present nightmares. He helped me improve my relationships with my family and friends. He helped me to begin accepting strangers as I hadn't in years. Dr. Charles Carluccio was my savior who saved my life.

After a few more moments of silence, Dr. Carluccio finally spoke.

"I think I'm starting to notice a pattern here. Do you have a thing against cops?"

I look up at him in disbelief. What does he mean by a "pattern"? The whole reason I was talking with him in the first place was because a PATH sergeant, who is basically an officer, sent me there. But as I eased back into my chair I quickly remembered a previous story, a true story, that I shared with him that might make him draw that conclusion. But in that story, everything based on misunderstandings and assumptions. Things are not always like that.

CHAPTER TEN

FDNY Reflections

I was a *proby*, or a first year probationary firefighter fresh out of fire school, in my Mid-Town Manhattan firehouse, Ladder 4. We got a call to respond to a fire in an attached tenement, five-story tenant walk-up only a few blocks away from the firehouse. It was around 7:30 at night, and this was the time that almost everyone in New York is on 46th Street, the same street where the fire is, because the theatres are open. The famous New York performances were underway at the same time that the "Pride of Mid-Town" needed to get to a performance of its own. No matter what it takes, we were not going to miss this fire, because even our firehouse motto was, "Never Miss a Performance."

So our chauffeur drove the truck the wrong way down 8th Avenue towards the 46th Street intersection so that we could be the first firehouse to reach the scene. We drove six blocks in the wrong direction and made a right turn that landed us right in front of the building. Now, I happened to be sitting behind the chauffeur because I had the *can*-which meant I would stay with the officer and carry the fire extinguisher when we went into the fire. So when it was time for me to get out, I was on the side of the street facing the steps leading up to the front double doors of the building.

We rushed in and headed towards the open door apartment door with smoke pouring out of it. Like so many Manhattan apartments, it was a tiny apartment and from the doorway we were already able to see the source of the smoke. It was a dinner gone wrong and everything on the stove top was smoking. It didn't help that the old building had raggedy cabinets that didn't do well when licked by flames from a kitchen fire.

Now Jack Guerci's job was to get to the roof and create a vent for the fire to move towards to avoid a situation where the flames reach out towards the very firefighters who were holding the water hose because it had nowhere else to run from the water. This meant that Jack had to trudge his way to the top of the huge, huge building to make sure none of us down below got into any trouble.

So he would probably take the adjoining building and jump the roof or take the aerial ladder to the roof. But running up the stairs is a lot faster than waiting for the aerial ladder to get set up. Now, I didn't see what was going on because I was on the right side and Jack was on the left side. He was supposed to be heading to the roof. The fire was almost out, but there was still gray smoke in the hallway. The fire was in a tiny studio apartment that only allows you to take two steps in before you hit the back wall.

There really wasn't any room to move in this place, so I stood in the hallway and straddling the threshold of the door while the other guys opened up the window, pulled the stove out and did whatever they needed to so they could maneuver. The officers talked to the guy who lived in the apartment and I was near the stairs. From there I could look all the way down the 40 foot hallway and through the vestibule, or the small six foot by four foot area with the mailboxes that sat between the outside door and the door to the inside of the building, and I saw Jack Guerci. I heard him arguing with these two guys that looked like thugs. One guy was really tall, about six foot six-the kind of guy you have to climb a ladder to punch- and I can hear all of them as they screamed and I just knew something was about to happen.

I didn't know if I had the *can* in my hand, but I guess I dropped it and I fell down on the wet slippery floor. I quickly got back up and started running towards Jack because I knew everyone else was in the building and I was the only one who could see what was going on. I wasn't going to leave him out there alone. I blasted through the first door and I could hear the yelling getting louder and I saw Jack and the big guy squared off and the little guy positioned himself like he wanted to catch Jack off guard and hit him while he was focused on the big guy. I dove right through the door onto all of them.

I tackled the little guy, because Jack's got the big guy, and we go right into the garbage pails! We grappled and wrestled and squared off. I grabbed this little guy and as his coat opened up allowing me to see a gold badge hanging from his neck. I wasn't used to seeing cops wear it around their necks like that. So while I was lying on the floor between Jack and this big guy and grabbing onto this little guy I looked up the steps towards Jack and yelled, "Jack! These guys are cops!"

It seemed like I said it in slow motion in a Sam Peckinpaw western because at that same moment Jack punched the big guy with a shot that sent blood all over the white tile. He almost knocked this guy out with one shot! I didn't know what was going on at this point, but I knew that the big guy was still trying to hold him and the little guy had a gun and was trying to hold him too. My focus at the time was on holding down the little guy and keeping him and his gun off of Jack.

Apparently this all started when we first arrived. The chauffeur went the wrong way down the street just so we could get to the fire. Jack got off the rig on the street side and I got off on the sidewalk side. We knew we had a fire and we needed to vent the roof, so the firehouse Baby Huey, Jack, was the one who got that assignment. I took off running through the building with the officers who moved like jack rabbits to see who needed to be rescued inside and find the fire. So Jack was left alone outside. When Jack opened the door to get out, there was a black unmarked cop car squeezing him as he opened the door. So he ripped the side view mirror off and threw it towards the car so he could get by and get to the roof. They hit the brakes, got out of the car and the guy pulled a gun on Jack! Now, Jack didn't know who he was, but the detective was dressed in a black leather trench coat like the Irish mafia wore at that time and pulled a gun on him. The first thing Jack thought of is not that this guy is a cop, but that this guy may be in the mafia. Jack slapped the guy's hand that was holding the gun as if he were saying "Get this thing out of the way, I've got to get to the roof and I have no time for you or your gun!" And apparently I showed up right after that.

And now this cop that Jack hit was crying, "I want that guy's job, I want him locked up!" Now there are nine more cops responding to a code 1013 that means there's a cop in trouble. That's a code that sends other cops flying towards the scene. The fire department chiefs were coming in and more fire trucks were coming in and I just knew there was going to be a huge mess on our hands.

As everyone showed up I was still lying on the floor and I was not letting go of this guy. Suddenly he started crying like a little girl as he points at Jack, "He hit me!" I couldn't believe that this guy who was trying to tear my head off a few minutes earlier was now crying like a victim. Both officers were taken to Bellevue Hospital. One of them may have had a broken nose. No charges were pressed against me, but Jack ended up in lock-up.

We finished the job and had a few more calls that night, so it was 6 am before we showed up at the precinct with the rig to pick him up. We had to work our way through the news teams in front of the firehouse that wanted exclusive interviews just so they could have more information than what was already in the newspaper headlines for the day.

When I walked in I saw him sitting there smoking his favorite Chesterfield cigarettes while there were three other guys huddled up together in the corner of the cell. I don't know what happened over the course of the evening, but it was clear that they didn't want any part of Jack. He had been in a cell before, I'm sure. And the fact that the cops didn't even take the handcuffs off him spoke volumes!

The chief started talking to him like he was a five-year-old about what he shouldn't be doing! By now you got news teams taking pictures of him in handcuffs that would go hand-in-hand with a story that some fireman in Brooklyn had a fight with a cop!

We had Jack on a modified assignment until everything blew over. I remember there was talk about a court date, but nothing came out of it as far as I knew.

I guessed it was this story that made Dr. Carluccio think I had a thing against cops, but that's not the case. I'll admit that I was amazed by how Jack fought that day. That punch that Jack gave was like being next to Mohammed Ali and Joe Frazier! What a shot! One shot, just one! But as the son of a retired NYPD officer and the friend of many other officers, I can't say that I have anything against all cops, it was just those particular cops that day that went after my firehouse brother, Jack.

Maybe I should I have told him about the time I went to lunch with Petey, a highway patrol officer. Judy and I both count Peter Ferrara as our best friend. He was even my best man at our wedding. Pete grew up around the corner from me on 69th St. and 19th Ave. I have known him since I was 12 years old. We have been so close for so long that he has been referred to as my mom's sixth son.

It was either Da Vinci's on 18th Ave. or L & B Spamoni Gardens, those were the final lunch choices for the day as Petey quickly wielded his sporty 380 Z when we left my house on Bay 37th Street in Bensonhurst Brooklyn. As we passed Mama Mia's pizza on Bath Avenue, only two blocks away from our destination, I was tempted to tell Pete to pullover the Z-car just for a quick slice that would put a dent in my tremendous hunger pangs. I got up early and I only had coffee throughout the day to sustain me, so now that it was about 3 o'clock I was starving! I decided against it knowing that Pete's expert driving skills would have us safely in front of Da Vinci's in a few quick minutes. I still couldn't resist prodding him to maximize his NYPD highway cop experience and put the pedal to the metal. If he had lights and sirens on his rocket ship I would have turned them on myself.

While riding past Mama Mia's I eagerly looked inside to see if Mario was pulling out a fresh pie from the oven and if he was I definitely had to ask Petey to stop by. But as I straightened my head to look forward again something strange caught my eye in the nanosecond it took to cross Bay 35th St. I thought I saw an all too familiar sight of heavy black smoke way down the block. I immediately hollered at Pete to stop with all the urgency of having just run over Miss America. The Z-car abruptly stopped.

"I thought you were starving, what's up?"

"Quick backup! We have to take a look down Bay 35th St.," was the only explanation I offered.

He quickly responded and a few seconds later he was speeding down Bay 35th St., a one-way street, in the wrong direction. People were in the street and on the sidewalk screaming as flames and black smoke permeated from out of the open front door and the top floor of the two story attached brick building. Pete quickly pulled the Z-car over across the street from the burning building in an unofficial parking spot that blocked someone's driveway.

We rushed across the street and up the steps of the stoop and into the open door while women and children outside were screaming that there were children trapped upstairs in the burning apartment. I didn't have time for even a quick size-up through the black smoke that met us immediately in the vestibule area, so I relied on what I knew about the buildings in this area. I knew the steps would be to the left even though I couldn't see them. As we bolted up the stairs we heard the screaming and crying of kids at the top of the stairs.

Thank God one of the kids, a petrified and crying little girl about four years old, was at the top of the steps waiting on us. I quickly grabbed her and handed her to Pete at the top of the stairs before I crawled on my belly past a burning room just a few feet away from the top of the stairs. I saw another child in the hallway laying on the floor just in front of me. The girl looked like she was about six years old and she was coughing and crying. When I finally reached her I scooped her up and crawled back to Pete and handed off the second child. I told him to get downstairs and out of the burning smoky building.

In the distance I heard sirens and knew that help was on the way. I attempted and successfully crawled into a rear bedroom that had the door open. The orange flames lit the room up enabling me to get a good view. I was blessed that the fire was already venting through the open windows in the rear of the room. I was able to search and look in and under the bed and take a quick look in the closet before my seared lungs burned with such intensity that I knew I was totally spent. So I crawled headfirst to the top of the stairs and slid down as Pete reentered the building.

"Get the hell out of there!" he yelled as he clambered up the stairs and pulled my outstretched arm, dramatically increasing the speed of my sliding retreat. He had been informed by the people on the street that there was no one left inside other than me. Pete had placed the two children safely in the custody of a neighbor's home directly across the street from the flame enveloped building. We knew if we didn't get the car out of the driveway we would be trapped by the incoming rigs responding to the fire from both directions on the one-way street. So we dashed back to the Z-car and Peter just pulled out of the block as one of the first to arrive was headed our way and narrowly passed the charging first due Engine that was racing to the fire.

When the fire-charged adrenaline gradually subsided, my attention once again returned to the void in my stomach. I inhaled that first square of delicious Da Vinci's pizza so quickly that it barely touched my lips. I started working on the second one probably about the same time that the first due Engine 253 "Bensonhurst's Bravest" Company we passed had finally extinguished the fire. I smiled to myself as I reflected on the moments leading up to our casual lunch. Great job, Brother Pete!

I had only written my "Teddy the Firebug" story because it was something Dr. Carluccio himself had recommended as part of my therapy. He challenged me to write stories as a way for me to get used to expressing myself again. I had pretty much shut down after being ostracized by my FDNY brotherhood. What else was I supposed to do after about half of the people I had known throughout my adult life were killed in the collapse of the twin towers and the rest of the people I knew didn't want to be bothered with me because they saw me as a robber of widows and orphans? After all of that I can't say that I was exactly an open and trusting guy.

"Well I'm glad to know that you don't have anything against cops," Dr. Carluccio stated as he interrupted my thoughts. "But are any of the events in your story true?"

Now that was a good question. There were a lot of crazy things that have happened in my firehouses over the years. And like any writer normally does, parts of the story were definitely gleaned from actual events. For example, Bobby Fash had a few things in common with Teddy.

When I became a firefighter, I had just moved to a brand new apartment, it was three stories, brand new buildings under the Verrazano Bridge, right on the water on Shore Road. My girlfriend and I lived on the top floor. When you're a firefighter candidate, like in the police department, you wear a different kind of uniform and you have a carryall bag, and they know you're going to school. The cop uniforms are usually gray, and in the fire department you have the same thing. So as I run into the building there was a guy on his way out who turned to looked at me and asked, "Hey, how you doing?"

"Hey, how you doing?" I replied, "You live here?"

"Yeah, I'm living here,"

"Oh, that's cool, you work out in Manhattan?"

"Yeah, I work in Manhattan."

"What's your name?"

"Bobby Fash."

"Oh, cool. Where are you?"

"I'm in *Proby School.*"

"Okay, cool."

And that was the end of the conversation. He was moving out, so I only saw him once or twice. I didn't know if he was getting divorced at the time, I really didn't know what the story was. But he had the studio apartment on the first floor and I had the big apartment on the third floor. All I knew was that I met him while I was in *Proby School* and when I got out and walked in the door of 4 Truck, where I was assigned, I saw the same guy I met in my building-Bobby Fash. He's in the firehouse! He's assigned to Ladder 4 with me!

And he was a Rockaway guy, he was a great swimmer, he grew up on the beach in Rockaway and he could swim for miles in the ocean. He was a real nice quiet guy with a barrel-chest who was strong as an ox. I wondered how fast he could knock down doors. The guy was tough!

He was not a good drinker though. One day when he was not working he went to a nice Irish bar right across the street from the firehouse where we used to cash our paychecks. It was more like a dive with the classic dirty windows, smoky atmosphere and old furniture. But as long as they served alcohol no one cared about all that. All the off-duty firemen went there to cash their check, drink and hangout. That is exactly what he was doing up at the bar.

I was scheduled to come in the next morning so I wasn't at the house or in on the payday bar crawl. When I parked across the street for my morning shift I noticed that the big old, wooden doors on this bar looked like they were hacked and the bar was entirely boarded up. I immediately assumed that they had a fire. I didn't smell the remnants of a fire, but what else could it be?

As I walked through the firehouse I noticed that everybody had this deadpan expression. This is when I knew something terrible happened. I asked over and over what was going on and all I heard in response was "Umhmm. Umhmm. Don't want to be the first one to tell you." By this point I absolutely had to know what was going on. Since no one was telling me anything, I started to make the coffee. As the rest of the guys gradually started talking I just outright demanded to know what is going on.

"You know Bobby Fash," one of the senior firemen asked me.

"Yeah, Bobby Fash what?" Now I was worried that he may have been injured on a call.

"Bobby Fash was in the bar last night," he sighed with a matter-of-fact voice, "with everybody else. I don't know if he stayed with his friends, or a couple of friends, and maybe one was a cop which was fine, I don't know. So at some point they turned to Bobby Fash and they're like, 'You're cut off. You're done.'"

What was great about that is if one of the guys was drinking and he lived far away, he could always sleep in the firehouse. No one really cared if he was there and it wasn't his tour, as long as he wasn't interfering with the guys who were on at that time. We did it all the time. You go to a ball game, or a party or a hockey game and you get out late, so you go to the firehouse so you won't have to drive. It wasn't a written rule or departmental policy, but we were all aware of that perk. So that is naturally where I assumed Bobby Fash ended up, but that wasn't exactly the case.

As the story goes, they tried to throw him out.

"You ain't throwing me out! My money's good!" Bobby yells at the bartender.

Mike's going, "Go ahead, you got to get out, no more drinking, you told me only one more!"

"Oh, no!" Bobby shouted back.

And then they tried to throw him out. This big guy tried to force him out of the bar but Bobby started fighting with him. Finally, they threw Bobby out the door, and they locked the door behind them. By now it's four o'clock in the morning which is the normal closing time for bars in Manhattan.

"I ain't done drinkin'!" Bobby shouted back.

Bobby eventually walked off towards the firehouse and the other firemen who were with him took off and went home. They all assumed that everything is settled for the night. But what did he do? He went into the firehouse and took the axe out of the rig and he went back across the street to try and chop the door down! Before he managed to get completely through the door cops arrived and locked him up!

He was a quiet guy! He never had words with any guy, kind of soft-spoken, not opinionated. Not one of the guys you would expect to pull a stunt like that. I didn't know he was a nasty drunk.

The bar didn't press charges but they did make him pay for the doors. Obviously, he was not allowed to come back into the bar. And everybody made believe it didn't happen. Or at least we didn't until the firehouse phone started ringing with calls from the other firehouses, "Hey, man, is Bobby Fash around?"

"Yeah, right! He's right here," the house watchman covering the phone would answer.

"No, he's across the street having a drink. We want our axe back!"

They were clowns. We even had a firehouse from down the street block their number and call us to say, "Well, tell him when he gets out of jail, to bring the axe back!" And that's the way that went! He still worked with us even though he got locked up, for ten minutes.

But I guess you could say that I got some of my story about Teddy from actual events, even if they didn't necessarily involve me. Dr. Carluccio asked me a few other questions about the Teddy story and then we moved on to other topics.

"Did most of the firefighters you were closest to spend time in lock up?" Dr. Carluccio asked without looking up from his clipboard.

Oh no, I could see where this was going. The colorful stories that involved lock up are usually the easiest to remember, and that's why I ended up sharing them with him first. It's not like everyone I associated with ended up in lock up. Even those who did were still good people who just made some poor decisions and were caught. But I could tell that I needed to set Dr. Carluccio straight on that, and soon. So I told him about a few of the guys I met throughout the years who I looked up to.

Bobby Gunn, sung "Danny Boy" the best I ever heard it. He used to make the bar cry when he sang a cappella. He held your attention whether you liked the song or not. He used to go into the bar across the street and after he threw down more than a few cold ones and his nose was nice and red like Rudolph the Red Nosed Reindeer, the 50-year-old Engine guy just started singing while the bar was packed! It wasn't one of those dainty martini joints. And all these old Irish guys, oh, he'd take the bartenders from the other side, that's the joint. You know, the Westies were tough, the west side was all like that. The bar went silent on two notes!

There were about 100 guys in there and not one of them made a sound! These guys were standing like they were at attention! They were just listening. He could sing the song with the best voice you ever heard. I had never even heard of the song and I started to wonder what it was but I didn't say anything because I know someone would be ready to slap me! He was singing this song, and the guys were crying!

He didn't do it all the time, he really didn't. People would ask him to perform it but he would never sing it. It had to be in the right moment. I caught it a few times, and he would sing it at functions and what not. Since I first heard him sing it, I have heard other guys sing it a million times, but Bobby's version is still the best I ever heard. Man, he could sing!

Bobby's part time job was working as a bank teller. He later was promoted to bank manager when he retired from the FDNY, but that guy had serious talent as a singer.

Mike Wernick was another guy who had talent. Wernick was the guy that went to Columbia Architect School's graduate program to become an architect while he worked in the biggest firehouse in the world. He was a Jewish guy. And he was a wrestler in college, back in the day. He was a little guy, a tough guy and an all-around great guy. He used to stay up all night with pots of coffee in the basement while he built these little models and then took his tests. He eventually became a full-fledged architect while he was a firefighter.

He lived in the village. He was a cool guy, married an Oriental girl, Nuri, she was from the Philippines. No kids, real nice guy. He was one of my best friends-a really great guy. He was my conscience, "you can't do that," he used to tell me. He was a calm, quiet guy, real easy-going. Good guy. Smart. And he lived in the village around the corner from Hell's Angels on the lower East Side before it was trendy, and then he moved around the corner, and here's the deal. He managed the only indoor motorcycle parking garage in the whole City of New York as his second job.

Some guy owned it, but he ran it. And he lived above it. It was a loft and it was very beautiful. There was an open deck out in the back that had French doors. He really made this place wonderful. Now it was quiet, and you'd never hear these motorcycles rustling or making any noise. He used to take me through there to show me some of the most beautiful motorcycles. A lot of heavy hitter musicians' bikes were there. I don't know if Bob Dylan's motorcycle was in there, but there were big heavy duty people who brought their bikes in, whether they used them or not.

And what you noticed about it, you weren't allowed to wash your bike and you weren't allowed to start your bike inside. You had to wheel it outside. He had all these rules. The place was called "Rising Wolf Motors." And everybody had their helmets and jackets and stuff. You couldn't work on the bikes in there, either. No oil changes or any of that. But everybody had a locker, like in the firehouse. All open. Nothing was closed and nobody stole anything. He had to have about 100-150 motorcycles in there. This was on both sides of the building, front to rear, big place. As of the time that this book is written, it still exists! In fact, he ended up buying the business and the building! He's an architect and a firefighter who happens to run a motorcycle shop. The guy is unbelievable! Unbelievable!

Now I think he wants to build a building above the building to give him more space. It's a good thing that he knows an architect who could design something like that.

Mike was also a 9/11 survivor. When I transferred to Brooklyn, he transferred the 9 Truck on Great Jones Street so he could walk to work. He told me that it was about 143 steps total. They had the biggest firehouse in the city, or one of them. They had the longest pole in the City, one from the third floor to the first floor. You had to be careful with that one. Oops! That was a huge firehouse! And they had these giant stalls in the basement that were their lockers. I mean giant stalls that were more like rooms. Mike had his architecture books and papers in there on a desk. His room even included lamps, chairs, and a couch. It was amazing!

He kind of did his work at the firehouse. But a brilliant guy, what a great guy! He drove the truck for Ladder 9. The truck was severely damaged, but it was not one of the trucks that were crushed. A couple of guys in the company that he worked with died, but he survived.

I remember going to a couple of tough fires with Mike. He was a very good firefighter. He made his bones in Brooklyn's Engine 207, but then he turned to the dark side and went to Midtowns 4 Truck. The guy was smart. He was always all in with the big guys who would pull the ceilings, force the doors and everything else that had to happen but he's a strong guy, real good shape, always in great shape. He also responded to the Trade Center bombing in '93. So his Ladder was probably second or third *due* down there. Operating in undetermined chaotic conditions was common place that these professionals masterfully took in stride.

I took my kids to Mike and Nori's and they were both in shock by the motorcycle collection. "He is so cool," they said as they went up to Mike's apartment. His wife is a professional masseuse and she specializes in prenatal. She had the room set up like an old Chinese pagoda kind of thing. And when you went in the kitchen you saw this big wooden deck that went out over the back of the garage. It's a really, really nice place in the east village. He's a great guy. Mike and his wife Nori took motorcycle trips all over the world. They've been on every continent!

There were plenty of firemen who trained for and worked second jobs as plumbers, technicians, contractors, and even lawyers, but he was the first and only firefighting architect I ever met.

Now that I had convinced Dr. Carluccio that everyone I socialized with during my firefighter days wasn't a convict, he wrapped up our session and I headed home.

Dr. Carluccio was the first psychiatrist I visited but he wasn't the last. Since 2002 I have shared my story with therapists who helped me get past the debilitating and severe depression and extreme pangs of loneliness so that I can pick up the pieces and keep going. It has been a process of reinvention. And although I was not Teddy the Firebug, with the path I was on before I started seeing the psychiatrist I could have ended up like Teddy.

It was Dr. Carluccio who was the determining factor that helped me to move forward and face my challenge of riding in traffic tunnels and bridges. Without facing this fear, I never would have been able to become one of the volunteers at the Tribute Center. They started talking about it in 2003. Because the official memorial would not be complete until 2009, the Tribute Center was being promoted as an "interim destination" where members of the 9/11 community, which included the survivors, residents, rescue and recovery workers, volunteers and family members, would be able to tell their personal story to visitors in conjunction with details on the fight to reach the 2,973 lives that were lost on that day. The advertised mission was to inspire healing, and that was something I too was in need of. I needed to be a part of Tribute, and Dr. Carluccio helped make that possible for me.

I had not returned to that site since January 6, 2002 when I left kicking and screaming wanting to stay until I felt my job was done, but it was not my decision to make. However it was my decision to return and share the stories of my friends and what happened to them on that fateful day. It was my decision to speak to the thousands of visitors who were projected to go through Tribute each day and explain what I had seen, what my role was there and what had I experienced. Most of all, It was my decision to be there to thank them for their blessings and their support for all of us that had taken part in America's history. Unbeknownst to them, it was their love and support that got me through the toughest times while I worked at Ground Zero. I needed to personally thank them. I needed this to help me heal too.

CHAPTER ELEVEN

Rising from Ashes

At first it was very difficult for me to become a docent for Tribute Center at Ground Zero. It took a lot just to muster up the courage to return to the scene of the crime, not to mention the drive to get there from New Jersey. It was very emotional for me to personally thank all of the people for their support. One person I was especially interested in thanking was a fearless woman by the name of Kimberly Krieger who I had first met in the days immediately following the collapse of the towers.

She had left her full-time job so that she could spend her days and evenings there at Ground Zero to serve the rescue workers as a Red Cross volunteer. I saw her each time I went to one of the recovery stations to get oxygen or water. She was always there to give us food, water, a blanket, someone to talk to, or whatever we could possibly need. I had participated in the Ground Zero rescue and recovery from September 11th, 2001 to January 6th, 2002, and I saw her there every single day. So I should not have been surprised to see her working again with the Tribute Center.

To reconnect with the people who had helped me during the times that I needed it most was one experience, but to make the trip to come and see nothing but a giant hole in the ground was quite another. It was truly amazing. I couldn't do it as much as I wanted to due to the emotional toll it took on me. But with the constant and persistent counsel and encouragement of Dr. Carluccio, it became a good part of my therapy.

Just before the Tribute Center opened I agreed to take smaller steps that would help me start to get out of the house before I took the big step of volunteering at Tribute. I joined something called the Optimist Club. It was my local chapter of a worldwide organization that was dedicated to serving the communities we lived in. We would raise money to send children with cancer to a one-week summer camp where they could get out of the hospital rooms where so many of them spent most of their days and enjoy spending time doing activities that would make them smile. They would be allowed them to interact with other children while they still had access to a 24/7 team of 9 on-duty volunteer nurses and an oncologist.

Not only did I help raise money to send 50 youths, up to age 17, to the camp, but I also spent my last week of June 2006 serving on the security team. The kids were always in groups of at least two and there was always a counselor with each of them. During the camp they had the opportunity to experience everything that their diagnosis permitted-from riding in hot air balloons, to zip lining, to participating in a game show, to watching performances of professional jugglers and demonstrations by animal handlers. It was amazing and I was so happy to be a part of it that I continued working with the program for at least two more years.

For almost three decades I adopted children in need through World Vision, but there was something special about being able to actually be there at those summer camps with the children that was really special. The experience even made me think about saving money so that I could travel out to Africa to visit with one of my adopted children. But after I calculated the cost of the travel, I thought it best to simply use the money to adopt another child somewhere and make a difference in another life instead of spending thousands to travel to a country and spend a few hours with a child who would probably be nervous and apprehensive about communicating with me. So I ended up doing just that, adopting another child in South America, and being content with sending letters and reading the ones that they wrote to me.

These experiences taught me how powerful giving is to the healing process. But it was an adventure I had in Philadelphia that showed me another side of giving.

My wife and kids were out of town and my mind buzzed with the possibilities of what to do. This was a freedom I had not experienced in a while. I took my last two nickels that I had saved for a rainy day and decided that it was finally pouring and time to shoot the wad! My lifelong favorite team, the NY Rangers, is an arch rival of Philadelphia and was about to play them for the top spot in the division. The Flyers were undefeated at home that season and I knew this was going to be a sold out game.

After a two hour drive to Philadelphia, I arrived with the hope of buying a single ducat. I knew enough to keep my lucky Rangers jersey under wraps just long enough to procure a ticket. There was no sense in letting the ticket scalper know that I was not a local. That would raise the price astronomically if they suspected that I came from NY to attend the game. I was blessed to find a legal parking spot on the street very close to the arena and saved $20 on a paid parking lot.

This left me with more funds for ticket negotiations. They were beginning to love me in Philadelphia.

As I walked through the parking lot I spotted a bona fide ticket agent hiding in the shadows.

"Tickets," he whispers.

"What you got? I only need one," I said.

"...Sec. 107 behind the goal. Row 13. Gimmie a buck and a quarter."

"Forty bucks," I quickly responded as I started to walk past him. I knew that I would have to be sharp.

"Seventy five," he shot back.

"Only got a fifty. Who wants it? I don't care where the seats are I just want to get in," I screamed. I also reminded him that there were only 12 minutes left until face-off.

"Done deal," he quickly concluded to avoid losing a sale to another scalper.

I made a silent exchange after examining the validity of the tickets. Sec. 107. Row 13. Seat 3. Directly behind the Ranger goal with an $89 face value. I chose that time to reveal my lucky Rangers jersey that commemorated the season '93-'94 Stanley Cup Championship win. The first time I boldly wore it was to the game seven Finals on the enchanted evening in June '94 when I witnessed the 54-year drought come to an end as the New York Rangers finally won the Stanley Cup. It was now the lucky Rangers jersey that I wore again to the game in Philadelphia.

"Thanks brother!" I said to the bewildered scalper who just learned that I had gotten the better of him.

And with that, the true blessing began. I could now profess the meaning of the City of Brotherly Love!

You have not completely experienced life as sports fan if you have not been to a major rival game in the insanely crazy hometown of Philadelphia while proudly wearing your team colors, the enemy's colors. The vile profanity, rage, anger, threats, and gestures were only multiplied as I chanted, "Let's Go Rangers," over and over again while I was deep in the Flyers lair.

As I descended to find my seat, the furious Flyer fans screamed at the top of their lungs in an effort to drown me out. This was aided by an aerial assault of peanuts and partially full beer cups that mysteriously only managed to hit me and not the people around me. Not at all bothered, I turned and welcomed the onslaught.

The first period ended in a typical hard fought and knuckle crushing one-all tie. Between the periods I was able to catch a fan favorite t-shirt fired off the ice by a beautiful Flyer cheerleader. By this time I knew they loved me in Philadelphia. I shared my new rolled up t-shirt love story with all who were within earshot.

The second period ended in a two-all tie. During the second stanza intermission there was an announcement over the public address system that all fans sitting in Sec. 107 won a remote controlled car courtesy of the Flyers.

"Go to Gate 120 and show your ticket stub to collect your prize."

I did just that, and now that I had scored free parking, a $35 savings on a ticket right behind my team's goal, a t-shirt and a remote controlled car. I knew that they loved me in Philadelphia!

The official Flyer photographer followed me and photographed me as I accepted my new toy. I detected a particular disdain as he carried out his obligatory duties, but I was more concerned with a greater potential problem. My raging and close quartered neighbors had now had two periods of drinking under their belts, so I anticipated further attacks with their freshened artillery. The toy car came with a small box of batteries. I didn't mind being pelted with peanuts, but flying batteries would surely do damage.

Once I made it back to my seat I spotted a young boy who was wearing his Flyer jersey and was sitting beside his dad in Sec. 106 in the first and second seat off the isle. They missed winning the car by one section.

I introduced myself as a retired firefighter from New York City and handed him a small photo taken of me at Ground Zero on September 11th. I told him to be a true fan and to always be loyal to his team, the Philadelphia Flyers. He looked like he was about 9 or 10 years old, and I told him that I had become a Rangers fan when I was around that same age. I continued to tell him how I had endured the pain of the losses and the thrills of the wins for 40 years and how he too would experience that with his team. Then I gave him the remote control car and the t-shirt.

I turned to return to my seat and the Flyer fans who witnessed the brief encounter erupted into cheers that were as energetic as when the Flyers scored a goal! They accepted me as a good guy who simply wore the wrong jersey.

On my long drive back home I reflected on how great America was...and how great it was to have your team win 4-3 in an overtime shoot out in the opponent's hometown. That day I learned that Philadelphia really is the city of brotherly love and that there really is something powerful about giving to others.

The co-founders of the Tribute Center understood the power of giving back, and I was glad to be able, and mentally prepared, to do so. The $3.4 million facility was housed in a Liberty Street storefront that was once a deli directly across the street from the World Trade

Center and next door to an FDNY firehouse. It featured four galleries that introduced visitors to life on Radio Row before September 11th, offered information on the February 26, 1993 bombing attack on the World Trade Center, connected them with the people and events of September 11th, 2001 and gave them a chance to reflect on their own experience. It's a touching tribute designed and managed by the men and women whose lives were personally touched by that fateful day-and I was one of the men who was able to volunteer there.

On September 6, 2006, three years after the co-founders had the idea for the center, we had a private opening for the 9/11 community of survivors and family members of those who were murdered on that day. It was a solemn, tearful, yet somehow tranquil day as we gathered together to remember the lives we lost and embrace our lives as those who survived. We were all in various stages of healing, but being together made an impact that I hadn't anticipated. On September 20th it would be open to the public, but this day was for us.

On one of the tours I gave on that special day for the 9/11 community, I learned about a man in a red bandana who I will never forget. Each of the docents was assigned a different spot in the Center so that we could explain each section. Near where I was standing was Welles Crowther's picture and when his mother, father and sister came through the mother explained more of his story to me.

Welles had been a volunteer firefighter in his pre-college days in Nyack, New York-a stone's throw from Manhattan. But he was in the South Tower as an equities trader now that he had a degree from Boston College. After news of the first plane landing in the North Tower, an old college roommate had called him to check on him and learned that he was heading out of the South Tower following a building wide announcement. That was the last contact he had with family and friends, but he spent the last hour of his life helping others escape the South Tower after it too was hit. The people he helped didn't know his name. They only knew that he wore a red bandana. But when Welles' mother heard the reports of a man with a red bandana who had helped people escape, she knew that it was her son who had worn the red bandana since his father gave it to him as a six year old boy.

Following September 11th, Welles' father went to his Manhattan apartment to collect his personal belongings. While in the apartment, the father found a printed out and unsigned application for the New York City Fire Department that was still awaiting the inclusion of a college transcript. He was going to give up his career as an affluent equities trader to become a firefighting city employee.

Welles was a man who had gone to work as a pawn who was there to do the work his supervisors had for him, and ended the day, and his life, as a warrior. In a matter of moments he made up his mind to change his fate. He may have survived had he simply left the tower, but he chose to take the cards he was dealt and do something different with it.

In honor of his memory, his family started something called the Welles Remy Crowther Charitable Trust that benefits young people. Each year they host an annual golf classic. There are races, concerts, and a list of other events designed to bring awareness to different issues regarding the youth, tell more people about their son, and continue to make an impact like Welles did on September 11th.

Before the Crowther family left the Tribute Center on that special day for 9/11 family members, we exchanged contact information and offered to help each other in any way possible. I knew that they put a lot of work into their causes and raised a lot of money for kids, so they already had my attention. But when they called me and invited me to play, of all things, ice hockey for their cause there was no way I could turn that down.

Welles was a hockey player in high school and a lacrosse player at Boston College, so his high school team had the idea of having a reunion game and inviting Welles' college lacrosse team members to play as well. The Crowther family remembered me, and my love of hockey, and they let me have the honors of being the slowest and fattest player on the ice. I loved it!

We were broken down into two teams, the White Team and the Black Team. I was on the White Team and I even had my own jersey. I didn't keep the jersey, though. I gave it back to them so that they could auction it off. Anything that they could make money off of I wanted them to have. It wasn't mine anyway. Besides, I did manage to get a picture of me out on the ice waiting for the game to start. Both teams wore identical jerseys in different colors that said, "Welles Crowther" on them.

Everybody got on the ice wearing a red bandana at the beginning and we played a good game. The Black Team really gave it to my team, the White Team. But it was all for a good cause. The event was covered in the news and in the newspapers. I couldn't believe how much money they were able to raise just so that they could give it away. They even sold jerseys and hats that were signed by professional athletes. They were definitely noticed in their area and they did a lot in memory of their son, the guy who could have been a multi-millionaire but wanted to be a firefighter instead.

I volunteered as a docent at the Tribute Center for a couple years after I met the Crowther family and I met a lot of families who chose to do things in honor of their fallen loved ones, but none were quite like this family. You might even say that having the opportunity to meet them inspired me to do more in honor of my fallen firefighters and to represent them on any occasion where I could.

I was honored to be invited by the United States Navy to take part in the christening of United States ship LPD 21, *USS New York*-the newest concept in the modern Navy. This ship class was specifically designed to combat the kind of modern terrorism that ended the lives of 2,973 people on September 11, 2001. The christening was in New Orleans, Louisiana. Getting to New Orleans had been on my short list for some 30 years, but the christening finally pulled it all together for me. I had missed the road trip there with my uncle, his children, and my older brother Charles back in the summer of 1968, but this time I had to make it.

During the 45 minute bus ride from New Orleans to the shipbuilding yard in Avondale, Louisiana, I thought about my dad. He served aboard a liberty ship in the US Merchant Marine, a branch of the US Navy during World War II. I caught a brief glimpse of the ship as the bus rolled down the tree-lined hill past its checkpoints and got closer. The *USS New York* proudly wore the number 21 on her hull. That was the same year that my father was born.

Tears ran down my face as I gazed at the ship in all its honor and glory. Seven tons of steel debris from the World Trade Center had been brought here, melted down, and embedded into the spine of the ship's mighty core. The *USS New York* was specifically designed to transport and deploy 800 US Marines under the cloak of invisible stealth. Her latest state-of-the-art training drills during transport ensured that these brave warriors would be ready at a moment's notice to be deployed and armed to the teeth with all the necessary equipment that is stowed within the confines of the ship.

As the magnum sized champagne bottle cracked across her majestic bow, the flags, banners and streaming ribbons came alive as they danced to the Pipes and Drums of the FDNY and the sounds of the NYPD band. More tears flooded my eyes because I knew that ship would serve stealthily and swiftly. The insurgents who hid behind rocks and deep dug caves in faraway places would be overtaken. Not all too soon they would utterly regret that they took sides against the United States of America.

CHAPTER TWELVE

Chiefs, Pawns
& Warriors

Prior to September 11, 2001, one of the greatest things I had
ever done was to sneak into Madison Square Garden to
watch my beloved New York Rangers play for the 1993-1994 Stanley
Cup. The Rangers hadn't won the Stanley Cup in 54 years, since
1940. I desperately wanted to go to the game. I had no money, no
tickets, nothing that could have gotten me anywhere near that game.
They sold those tickets for a minimum of $2,500 to over $5,000 for
one seat anywhere in the building. I tried like heck. I knew I was off
that night. I was nervous for my team. I scrambled and I didn't know
what to do.

Then it had dawned on me that I had done hundreds and
hundreds of building inspections in Manhattan. I thought that I
could possibly pull this off if I put my Class A uniform on. I
borrowed a clipboard from the firehouse and put some old building
inspection paperwork, cards and guidelines from the office on it. It
was all official paperwork but it wasn't filled out for Madison Square

Garden and it would not be submitted like a real inspection. Now I was ready to go.

I knew I had to get there really, really early. Generally speaking, if the game starts at 7:30 or 7:00, you have to be in that building by about 4:30. I also needed to get in through the side entrance. Inspectors don't go through the gate to the front door, they go underneath the Garden where the players enter. There are all kinds of security down there and that's where the owners come in. It's really a big deal to get through. But once I had my Class A uniform and hat on and collected my official clipboard with the peach colored building card, I was confident that I would be able to lead the Garden staff to believe I was one of their official pre-game inspectors. Public venues are always inspected and this was a common occurrence for them, so the people in security expected the fire department to show up, as well as special details from the police department.

When I went in, I saw no less than two captains, three chiefs and a chief's aide that were going into the Garden. They were probably doing the same thing I was doing, except they got a free meal because of their rank. So I kind of piggy backed off of them. They didn't really see me because I came up from behind them, so I kind of waited to see when I could make my move. When they went through security they were met by a detail of Madison Square Garden officials to guide them and take them by the hand to where they had to go.

So they went into this bank of elevators and I kind of shortened the gap between us to make sure that I could still get in. All of a sudden a guy from the detail hosting the group of captains, chiefs and the chief's aide turns around looks at me.

"Is this guy with you?"

They all turned around and saw me in my Class A's and looked at me with puzzled expressions on their faces. But somehow the chief's aide remembered me. I only vaguely remembered him. He was an older guy who must have had at least 25 years on the job and I think he was a chief's aide in the 7th Battalion and I was in the 9th Battalion, so our firehouses couldn't have been too far away from each other. But the chief's aide actually called my name.

"Hey, Ron! Yeah, he's with us."

Just like that. And then he gave me one of those eye brow movements that told me that he was going to cover me to get me in but that I was not welcomed to go with them because he had already done what he could do for me.

I took the hint and I didn't get into the elevator with him, I took another one instead. I had to make believe that I was walking around the Garden checking exits. I didn't really care what I had to do because I was in the building now. I was in and had free reign. I didn't have a ticket or a seat, but it didn't matter.

Where do I go? It's about 4:45 and the game was not scheduled to start for at least 2 hours. The fans were not even let in yet. So I decided to go up to the lounge. I was never invited up there before because that's where the zillion dollar seats are. I found it after asking some of the workers I found pushing cleaning carts. So I took an elevator to go up a few more flights to reach the lounge area. Remember, once you get past security and you get into the building you have free reign because no one else is going to ask you what you are doing-especially if you're in uniform.

When I arrived I found a very large and very nice bar area and restaurant. I didn't have any money for that so I was not interested in staying. But while I was up there I ran into Mike Francesa, one of the most famous sports radio announcers. At the time he was a co-host on the popular "Mike and the Mad Dog" radio show. Now he has his own radio program. He was in the radio business for maybe 30 years and he was one of those people who was always at a major game like this.

"Hey, Mike! How are you doing?"

"Alright," he replies once he sees me.

Now all this time I carried a shopping bag with me. I sat down with Mike and chatted with him for a moment.

"The Rangers are going to win the Cup tonight," I proudly announced.

Mike just looked at me.

"I guarantee the Rangers are going to win the Cup. Look at what I've got."

I opened up the shopping bag and I showed him my brand new white NY Rangers jersey with the following words on the back, "Stanley Cup 1993-1994 Champs." It's falling apart now and I still have it, but that is what I showed him that day. I have worn it occasionally since then. In fact, it was the same jersey I wore when I attended the Rangers game in Philadelphia when I gave the tee shirt and the remote controlled car to the young lad.

Now I knew that the shirt would be garbage if the Rangers lost that night, but I had confidence. I also had a key ingredient in my bag next to the jersey. I had my ice skates with the special blade covers that were made out of old firefighter rubber boots. They were a key part of my plan. When the Rangers won the Stanley Cup, I was going to put the jersey on and put the skates on and wait until the Cup came out to go out on the ice with my team. I was going to grab the Cup as a fan favorite of New York City. I didn't care what was going on because that's what I was going to do. That was the major plan. But in the meantime, I knew that I needed a place to hide. So I said my goodbyes to Mike. I never spoke to him again after that, but I'll never forget having met him that day.

So I went around the Garden with my shopping bag and decided to look all the way upstairs where the skyboxes were for a seat. I knew these seats were impregnable and that you just couldn't get in there. There was security everywhere and I didn't know who any of these people were. I walked into one room and saw a lady sitting in the front row. I didn't recognize her, but I quickly learned that she was Emily Griffiths, the wife of the late Frank Griffiths who founded the Vancouver Canucks and the mother of Arthur Griffiths the Vancouver Canucks president. She saw me come in with my Class A's and she must have assumed that I had an official reason for being there.

"How are you? Come on in!" She invited me. Then she motioned for me to have a seat. I introduced myself and tried to get comfortable. It was unbelievable to get seats like this at the game, but I'm a Rangers fan and I couldn't watch the Stanley Cup game in enemy territory. Fortunately someone came in to give me the perfect excuse to leave.

A couple detectives in suits that prominently displayed their gold shields came in and looked right at me.

"What are you doing here?"

"I'm doing inspections," I respond nonchalantly.

"Listen, the Mayor is coming to sit in this box. You better get out of here."

They probably caught up to my act because there really was no reason for me to sit and stay in the box during rounds of "inspection" anyway. So I do the only thing I could do at the time.

"Ok, guys. Thanks a lot. I'll see you later," and I got out of there quick so I could look for another skybox to get into.

I walked around the upper ring where all these skyboxes were and I just turned door knobs and walked in to see what was going on. I kept running into people who really looked like stuffed shirt people who were there because it was the kind of event that it seemed like people with money should go to-not because they were really interested in the game itself. I could not crash with these people. They seemed like they were more interested in business and that really was a waste of seats. But after opening about three to four more doors my firefighter nose picked up on a smell that let me know that I had found a home.

I didn't smell fire, but I smelled pot and I immediately knew that no one in this room was going to get upset with me because I wasn't invited or didn't have a ticket. I walked in and closed the door and there were six or seven guys who turned around with their doobies and joints in hand and suddenly a look of fear entered their eyes.

"He's a cop!" One of them yells.

"No, no, no, no!" I reassured them, "I'm not a cop. It's cool. Everything is cool. Who cares? Hey guys, I have a problem. Is it alright if I hang out with you guys? I'm kind of doing this building inspection and the game is about to start."

"Yeah! Come on in! Have a drink! Do what you want. No problem."

So now that I had a spot, I put my shopping bag and my clipboard to the side and I was there partying with these guys in seats that may have cost $10,000 or more. I didn't know. But these were young Wall Street guys in their mid-30's and they were really partying. They ordered all this food and all these drinks. I couldn't tell you what it cost, but they partied the whole time.

I had told a few people in my firehouse, Ladder 148 that I was going to get into the game that night. I didn't tell them how, but I just knew I was going to get in. So when I saw the phone in the skybox, I called up the firehouse.

"Do you hear this?" I asked the fireman who answered the phone just before I turned the phone receiver so that it could pick up all the screaming from the fans that filled the Garden.

When I put the phone back to my ear I could hear Bobby Perretta shouting to everyone around him.

"He's in the game! I can't believe it. He's in the game!"

They were all really happy for me. I couldn't tell them how I did it though.

And the game was a nail bitter. Near the end of the game the Rangers were up by one goal and I decided that it was time for me to make a move.

"Hey, guys. I'm going to take off my uniform and put them in this bag. You give me one of your cards so I can reach you later."

I was at the top of the Garden so I had to run down the emergency exit with my skates on with a minute left in the game to reach the ice. I decided to put my jersey on over my uniform so that I would make it, so I put my shoes and my hat in the bag. When they saw my jersey they went crazy over it. After I told them my plan for getting my hands on the Stanley Cup to represent all the New York fans, they volunteered to be my backup.

"If you get locked up we'll bail you out. Don't worry about it!"

I hadn't thought about that possible outcome before they said it and I could have lived without them mentioning it, but I didn't let it deter me from my mission. I ran all the way down to the first level using the emergency exit stairwell and I approached the glass that is low enough for me to jump over, but while I was there I noticed something that I hadn't anticipated.

This was the first year that Mayor Giuliani was in office and he ordered the riot police to be placed all around the ice just before the end of the game to keep everything in check. People go crazy after Stanley Cup games. In some cities people loot, they blow up things, just all kinds of things tend to happen so he took the precautions he thought were necessary to keep everything in order. There must have been about 200 of them. I still tried to edge closer and closer to the ice. I finally got within 15 feet of the glass and I waited because my plan was to go out there after the Cup came out. People all around me screamed and I was ready to get out there on the ice and celebrate. I didn't care that the cops were there because I knew once I got out on the ice with my skates that they wouldn't be able to chase me on the ice with their shoes on. They would fly all over the place. I just had to get over that glass. I was going to be one of the first guys to get their hand on that Cup because we deserved it and I'm a die-hard Ranger's fan and the best fan in Madison Square Garden and this is as good as it gets. My plan was to either be on David Letterman the next night or in jail-in either case I was going to get my hands on that Cup.

While I got lost in my thoughts about what I was going to do next, I didn't realize that I happened to be standing next to the NYPD lieutenant who was in charge of the section where I was standing. He had a small detail of guys with him. Something about me caught his attention because he kept watching me. I tried to look forward nonchalantly like I didn't feel him looking at me, but when he finally looked down, my entire plan was ruined.

"He's got skates on!"

At this point I was 8-10 feet away but before I could even make a move towards the glass about four or five big cops grabbed me and threw me down on the ground. They didn't know if I was a terrorist or some other kind of crazy man. They only knew that I wore skates and that I had something planned that probably wouldn't be good news for them or their jobs. Once they pinned me down on the ground they started to rifle through my pockets.

"What's that?" He asked.

"That's my badge."

"Your badge? You're a cop?!"

"No, I'm a fireman."

"Hey, Lieu. This guy's a dopey fireman."

The lieutenant told them to stand me up so he could talk to me.

"There's no way you're getting on the ice. I'm getting promoted to captain in a short while and this will be a tremendous stain on my record if you jump on the ice. You can stand there, I'm going to have all these cops stand around you. But if you make a move I'm going to handcuff you and lock you up. No matter what!"

So I patiently waited a few extra minutes to watch them bring out the Stanley Cup. It was beautiful and I still enjoyed watching my team celebrate our victory. When I walked outside everybody was happy. There was no violence whatsoever. Everybody was hugging each other and high-fiving each other. I was ecstatic too!

By this time I still walked around in my ice skates because I had lost my shoes and my hat. I didn't lose the card I grabbed from one of the guys, but I did not remember how to get back to the skybox I had been in earlier and didn't know the skybox phone number so I could reach them to retrieve my belongings. I had more than a few beers in me at the time but I wasn't driving home and nothing at all seemed to matter. All the nearby bars were emptied which flooded the streets with thousands of additional revelers. Part two of this enchanted evening was about to start.

There were just so many people that celebrated on the Madison Square Garden plaza and in the street that I stopped several times to dance, hug or chest bump with everyone I met. Drivers and passengers left empty cars and taxis in a traffic jam in the street while they joined the fans in celebration. The air was filled with chanting, laughing, singing and the sounds of hundreds of popping champagne bottles.

I danced on 8th Avenue in my ice skates while I chanted "1940," and, "Let's Go Rangers"!

One fan's sign said it all, "NOW I CAN DIE IN PEACE." I had the best time of my life and it was one of the greatest things I've ever done.

But since September 11th, I've gained a new found passion that I'm even more determined about than I was that day to watch the New York Rangers, play in a final game seven and win the all too elusive Stanley Cup. I'm determined to make sure that people don't have the chance to forget the sacrifice and significance of September 11th, 2001 and the lessons we can learn from it on how we live our own lives.

What can we learn from 9/11?

As a nation, America's world almost fell apart with the devastation and destruction of the World Trade Center's two 110 story buildings, the five other buildings, and the destruction and demolition of the surrounding neighborhood, the disruption and shutting down of the New York City stock exchange, the annihilation and vaporization of over 100 long established businesses, not least to mention the broken families and missing loved ones. Fear and sadness still overwhelms me when I think about the unshakable and non-ending punishment and the tragic disappointment that fell on me when I returned to Dante's Inferno day after day in those days, weeks and months following September 11th. Hell is where I lived for some time. I became a reverse gravedigger by day looking for survivors and a zombie by night that wouldn't and couldn't sleep.

Imagine living with the hope of recovering a small remnant or a pulverized and emaciated fragment of a human cadaver that not too long ago belonged to an entire living and loving human. We would hope for a miraculous rescue by anyone at any time. We would hope that just one person would be found alive, possibly in a vault or in the safety of some other small crevice in the bowels of the building. And then watch over time that hope for finding someone alive diminished into the vaporous fog of ash of what still remained.

As a proud American citizen, this was the loss I shared, and continue to share, with every American who was alive on that day. But this was not the only loss I experienced in response to that day. My career nosedived into obscurity. The career of what I thought would continue for at least another 20 years. I had aspirations of passing the test to become an officer-a lieutenant. After that I planned to learn, teach and study a few more years to become a captain or even possibly someday the chief before I reached that second-tier of another twenty-year plateau. What was once a possibility for me was now an impossibility. Talk about a game changer. I was blindsided and my heart hung heavy, too heavy to quit. I was not a quitter. I'll never be a quitter, but my career was in the toilet. My world, as I knew it, was ripped from under me.

I lived out the next few years of working on Staten Island in total obscurity. Staten Island was the land of very few structural fires, the kind of fires I was groomed to handle. Staten Island was the home of car accidents and brush fires. I was no longer "Hammer," I had become Smokey the Bear.

I got my nickname "the Hammer" from fellow Trucker Wayne Smith while working with him in Ladder 4 in Manhattan. He gave me the name when he noted that I was a good irons man and could hit the hell out of a softball. I guess the name fit because it stuck with me throughout my career. I was officially the HAMMER.

It was not a bad moniker. There were many firefighters with real shitty nicknames that they had no control of. You didn't pick your own nickname. You earned it one way or another. I definitely came across some regrettable monikers that the owners didn't want and hated with a passion. Some of the names on that list include: Cock-a-pants, booze-bag, hair-bag, square-rooter, seagull, space-cadet, Pugsley, or the Fresh Air Man.

These names occasionally caused many an uproar leading to threats, fisticuffs, stabbings and sometimes all-out war within the house. Unofficial sit-downs were sometimes necessary to restore house order. When this happened, they were attended by company members ONLY and there was never any officer involvement. The senior men who had been in that house the longest ran the show and were highest on the pecking order.

I miss my brother Wayne Smith. Wayne was big, strong and very intelligent. He was also a Detroit Tigers fan. I could never quite figure out that one being a kid from Queens and living a stone's throw from Shea Stadium, surrounded by a borough of very loyal Met fans. Wayne, who was 6'4" weighing 220 pounds, was a soft handed first baseman that batted lefty. He had been a pitcher at St. John's University, also known for their great basketball program and their fine baseball team. New York Mets Hall of Fame pitcher John Franco also attended St. John's.

As a fireman, Wayne rose to the rank of lieutenant very quickly. I don't think he had 15 years on the job in total before he earned that rank which was a pretty amazing accomplishment and he certainly earned his promotion. But Captain Wayne Smith was killed in a hellacious fire on August 7, 1994 in the borough that bore him- Queens, New York. I visited him at the burn center in Manhattan after his wife and family had left. Wayne was never left alone, 24 hours a day there was someone by his side. I was met by Lieutenant Mike Mc'Glocklin, affectionately known as Opie, when the three of us worked together as firefighters at Ladder Company 4. Now Opie was a lieutenant in Ladder 138 in Queens. One of our brothers stood vigil. There was always someone from his house Engine 287, Ladder 136 as well as Engine 54, Ladder 4, Battalion 9- as well as the house of Engine 205, Ladder 110 where Wayne served as a lieutenant.

Opie had warned me before I entered the sterile setting of Wayne's room. I was shocked and frozen still as I looked at my good friend lying there. I saw what fire could do to even us, the well-trained. Wayne's face and head was burned and swollen beyond recognition. Wayne was a courageous fighter who fought to live.

He fought and lingered for 40 days and never opened his eyes from that terrible coma. Wayne finally succumbed because the noxious superheated air and flames seared his lungs on the inside that caused irreversible damage. Wayne's fight was fought.

Wayne's deadly fire was critiqued by the FDNY investigations unit with the conclusion that Wayne could have saved himself many different times throughout that job, but that Captain Wayne Smith of Ladder 110 simply chose not to. Captain Wayne Smith led his men into that raging inferno. He pushed forward through the deadly flames even after his mask was depleted of air that made matters critical and deadly. Without regard for the flames and searing heat, Captain Wayne Smith stayed and searched for one of his unaccounted members who, unbeknownst to Wayne, had already escaped.

If you ever had the pleasure of meeting Wayne Smith you would soon see that beyond his rugged exterior that he would quietly lay down his life for you. I was honored to be named" The Hammer" by Wayne Smith who is now the starting pitcher for Heaven's Detroit Tigers. But I had been reduced from a high-rise firefighter in Manhattan as well as an accomplished seasoned firefighter in the borough of fire, Brooklyn, New York, to a mere shell of myself exiled from the world I knew to the borough of Staten Island.

Until I found another purpose, I thought my life was over. Unfortunately, I know that I am not the only person who has ever found himself in a situation where their life as they knew it was suddenly under an attack that they could have never predicted.

We all heal in different ways. I am a very sensitive person and I don't think that I will ever completely heal. I will NEVER FORGET neither the attacks of September 11th or its aftermath that changed my career. Both still bring many emotions and great pain and suffering to this day. There are still firefighters and other emergency first responders who are dying today due to September 11th related respiratory illnesses and cancer. Even Billy O'Connor died of cancer about five years after the day we worked together to pull people from the rubble. This is something that I will carry with me until God calls me to heaven as a good and faithful soul. But there are three things that I have learned that definitely helped me with moving forward.

1. **Use whatever God has blessed you with to help and benefit someone else.**

Whether it is a special talent of yours that can help others, finances, your unique personality or even your ability to physically help someone out. Continuing to adopt children in foreign countries through World Vision, being part of the security team at a summer camp for children with cancer through The Optimist Club, sharing my story as a docent at the Tribute Center and speaking at several 9/11 memorial events over the years has gone a long way towards helping me make sense of what happened and giving me a new outlook on future possibilities. In fact, I hope to use the proceeds of the book in your hands to build a 9/11 memorial in Florida, the place that I now call home.

2. **Remember that someone else's unfortunate life is far worse and much graver than yours.**

Thank God that you have the voice and the ability to change your life for the better. As devastated as I was at the loss of my career, Welles Crowther was an incredible man who never had the chance to complete his career change from an equities trader to a fireman. I at least had the chance to enjoy my dream career for 20 years and I still have my life today so that I can continue to reach for new dreams.

3. **Never give up and move in a positive direction by taking just one step at a time.**

Seek professional help if you need to. I didn't want to start seeing a psychologist, but I still see one today to help me stay balanced and it is a decision that I will never regret.

In life, all of us have the choice to be a chief, a pawn or a warrior. In some instances you may be a chief and in others you may never want to shoulder that kind of leadership responsibility, and that's just fine. You may never want to be a Warrior but there may suddenly be a time when you rise to the occasion and masterfully transform into the hidden Warrior within you like thousands of us did on the search and rescue team following September 11th, or even as I did when I started the process of shrugging off the my depression long enough to start becoming an active participant in life again.

You may have been lead to believe that if you are a Pawn that it is not as desirable as the other two roles. Believe me, being a Pawn can be a wonderful thing. When you learn to be at peace with yourself and find contentment in where you are, you realize that this is a place where you are actively being protected by other warriors and chiefs around you. This was my role during much of my career as a firefighter. We always went into dangerous situations, but with being part of a great team where the chiefs and warriors stepped up as needed, my life as a pawn was always protected and the work I did helped the chiefs and warriors do a better job of protecting me. The same is true for you.

It is your God-given choice to change when and how to change between the roles because all are necessary to reach our life goals. Through hard work, determination, skill, knowledge, perseverance and drive, you will succeed and achieve your ultimate goal.

I know that I am all three-a chief, a pawn and a warrior. For the most part, I'm a pawn now in a relaxed state of mind-just relaxing and learning new things. Part of the reason I am so at ease with being a pawn is that I know I am trained to be a warrior and that I can transform in a moment's notice if I need to. Hopefully I'm not getting too long in the tooth, but I know that a true warrior lies hidden beneath this well rested body. Time has passed for me to aspire to be a FDNY chief, although I have witnessed and studied a great many chiefs in my lifetime. I respectfully thank them for their undaunted professional actions and their perseverance that has kept the brothers and me safe and alive so that we could return to our families again. I cannot thank them enough. But I still have not given up on the thought that there may still be other missions where I may be needed in the role of chief. If it happens, I'll be ready.

But my question for you is this: do you choose to be a chief, a pawn or a warrior? And notice that choosing to be a victim is never an option.

Watch your thoughts for they become words.

Watch your words for they become actions.

Watch your actions for they become habits.

Watch your habits for they become your character.

And watch your character for it becomes your destiny.

What we think, we become.

My father always said that...and I think I am fine.

-Margaret Thatcher

POSTSCRIPT

These are the first responders who we will "Never Forget" for their ultimate sacrifice on September 11, 2001.

RON'S GUYS

This list is according to the official list by the FDNY. Please note that any ranks with an asterisk were awarded posthumously.

FDNY Chief

Peter J. Ganci, Jr.

FDNY Assistant Chief

Gerard Barbara

Donald Burns

FDNY First Deputy
Commissioner

William M. Feehan

FDNY Fire Marshal

Ronald Paul Bucca

FDNY Chaplain

Father Mychal Judge

Battalion 4

Chief Matthew Lancelot Ryan

Battalion 2

Chief William McGovern

Chief Richard Prunty

Faustino Apostol, Jr.

Battalion 6

Chief John P. Williamson

Battalion 7

*Deputy Chief Orio Palmer

215

Battalion 8

Chief Thomas Patrick
  DeAngelis

Battalion 9

*Deputy Chief Edward F.
  Geraghty

Chief Dennis Lawrence
  Devlin

Carl Asaro

Alan D. Feinberg

Battalion 12

*Deputy Chief Joseph Ross
  Marchbanks, Jr.

Chief Frederick Claude
  Scheffold, Jr.

Battalion 48

Chief Joseph Grzelak

Michael Leopoldo Bocchino

Battalion 57

*Deputy Chief Dennis Cross

Engine 1

Lt. Andrew Desperito

Michael T. Weinberg

Engine 4

*Chief Joseph D. Farrelly

Calixto Anaya, Jr.

James C. Riches

Thomas G. Schoales

Paul A. Tegtmeier

Engine 5

*Lt. Manuel Del Valle

Engine 6

Paul Beyer

Thomas Holohan

William R. Johnston

Engine 8

Robert Parro

Engine 10

Lt. Gregg Arthur Atlas

*Fire Marshal Paul Pansini

Jeffrey James Olsen

Engine 21

Capt. William Francis Burke, Jr.

Engine 22

*Fire Marshal Vincent D. Kane

Thomas Anthony Casoria

Michael J. Elferis

Martin E. McWilliams

Engine 23

John Marshall

Robert McPadden

James Nicholas Pappageorge

Hector Luis Tirado, Jr.

Mark P. Whitford

Engine 26

*Chief Thomas Farino

Dana R Hannon

Robert W. Spear, Jr.

Engine 33

Lt. Kevin Pfeifer

David Arce

Brian Bilcher

Michael Boyle

Robert Evans

Robert King, Jr.

Keithroy Marcellus Maynard

Engine 37

John Giordano

Engine 40

Lt. John F. Ginley

Kevin Bracken

Michael D. D'Auria

Bruce Gary

Michael Lynch

Steve Mercado

Engine 52

Lt. Thomas O'Hagan

Engine 54

Paul John Gill

Jose Guadalupe

Leonard Ragaglia

Christopher Santora

Engine 55

Lt. Peter L. Freund

Robert Lane

Christopher Mozzillo

Stephen P. Russell

Engine 58

Lt. Robert B. Nagel

Engine 65

Thomas McCann

Engine 74

Ruben D. Correa

Engine 82

Lt. Geoffrey E. Guja

Engine 152

Robert Cordice

Engine 154

Capt. William O'Keefe

Engine 201

Lt. Paul Richard Martini

Greg Joseph Buck

Christopher Pickford

John Albert Schardt

Engine 205

Lt. Robert Francis Wallace

Engine 207

Karl Henry Joseph

Shawn Edward Powell

Kevin O. Reilly

Engine 214

*Lt. Carl John Bedigian

John Joseph Florio

Michael Edward Roberts

Kenneth Thomas Watson

Engine 216

Daniel Suhr

Engine 217

Lt. Kenneth Phelan

Steven Coakley

Philip T. Hayes

Neil Joseph Leavy

Engine 219

John Chipura

Engine 226

Brian McAleese

David Paul Derubbio

Stanley S. Smagala, Jr.

Engine 230

Lt. Brian G. Ahearn

Frank Bonomo

Michael Scott Carlo

Jeffrey Stark

Eugene Whelan

Edward James White III

Engine 235

Lt. Steven Bates

Nicholas Paul Chiofalo

Francis Esposito

Lee S. Fehling

Lawrence G. Veling

Engine 238

Lt. Glenn E. Wilkinson

Engine 279

Ronnie Lee Henderson

Michael Ragusa

Anthony Rodriguez

Engine 285

Raymond R. York

Engine 310

Capt. Thomas Moody

Engine 320

Capt. James J. Corrigan

Haz-Mat 1

Lt. John A. Crisci

Dennis M. Carey

Martin N. DeMeo

Thomas Gardner

Jonathan R. Hohmann

Dennis Scauso

Kevin Joseph Smith

Capt. Patrick J. Waters

Haz-Mat Operations

Battalion Chief John Fanning

Ladder 2

Capt. Frederick Ill, Jr.

Michael J. Clarke

George DiPasquale

Denis P. Germain

Daniel Edward Harlin

Carl Molinaro

Dennis Michael Mulligan

Ladder 3

Capt. Patrick J. Brown

Lt. Kevin W. Donnelly

Michael Carroll

James Raymond Coyle

Gerard Dewan

Jeffrey John Giordano

Joseph Maloney

John Kevin McAvoy

Timothy Patrick McSweeney

Joseph J. Ogren

Steven John Olson

Ladder 4

*Capt. Daniel O'Callaghan

Capt. David Terence Wooley

*Lt. Michael F. Lynch

Joseph Angelini, Jr.

Michael E. Brennan

Michael Haub

Samuel Oitice

John James Tipping II

Ladder 5

*Capt. Vincent Francis Giammona

Lt. Charles Joseph Margiotta

Lt. Michael Warchola

Louis Arena

Andrew Brunn

Thomas Hannafin

Paul Hanlon Keating

John A. Santore

Gregory Thomas Saucedo

Ladder 7

*Capt. Vernon Allan Richard

George Cain

Robert Joseph Foti

Richard Muldowney, Jr.

Charles Mendez

Vincent Princiotta

Ladder 8

Lt. Vincent Gerard Halloran

Ladder 9

*Lt. Jeffrey P. Walz

Gerard Baptiste

John P. Tierney

Ladder 10

Sean Patrick Tallon

Ladder 11

Lt. Michael Quilty

Michael F. Cammarata

Edward James Day

John F. Heffernan

Richard John Kelly, Jr.

Matthew Rogan

Ladder 12

Angel L. Juarbe, Jr.

Michael D. Mullan

Ladder 13

Capt. Walter G. Hynes

Thomas Hetzel

Dennis McHugh

Thomas E. Sabella

Gregory Stajk

Ladder 15

Lt. Joseph Gerard Leavey

Richard Lanard Allen

Arthur Barry

Thomas W. Kelly

Scott Kopytko

Scott Larsen

Douglas E. Oelschlager

Eric T. Olsen

Ladder 16

Lt. Raymond E. Murphy

Robert Curatolo

Ladder 20

*Capt. John R. Fischer

John Patrick Burnside

James Michael Gray

Sean S. Hanley

David Laforge

Robert Thomas Linnane

Robert D. McMahon

Ladder 21

Lt. Michael N. Fodor

Gerald T. Atwood

Gerard Duffy

Keith Glascoe

Joseph Henry

William E. Krukowski

Benjamin Suarez

Ladder 24

Capt. Daniel J. Brethel

Stephen Elliot Belson

Ladder 25

*Fire Marshal Kenneth Kumpel

Matthew Barnes

John Michael Collins

Robert Minara

Joseph Rivelli, Jr.

Paul G. Ruback

Ladder 34

Lt. Anthony Jovic

Lt. Glenn C. Perry

Ladder 35

Capt. Frank Callahan

James Andrew Giberson

Vincent S. Morello

Michael Otten

Michael Roberts

Ladder 42

Peter Alexander Bielfeld

Ladder 61

Lt. Charles William
Garbarini

Ladder 101

Lt. Joseph Gullickson

Patrick Byrne

Salvatore B. Calabro

Brian Cannizzaro

Thomas J. Kennedy

Joseph Maffeo

Terence A. McShane

Ladder 103

Capt. Timothy M. Stackpole

Ladder 105

Capt. Vincent Brunton

*Lt. Thomas Richard Kelly

Henry Alfred Miller, Jr.

Dennis O'Berg

Frank Anthony Palombo

Ladder 110

Lt. Paul Thomas Mitchell

Ladder 111

Lt. Christopher P. Sullivan

Ladder 118

Capt. Martin J. Egan, Jr.

Lt. Robert M. Regan

*Lt. Joseph Agnello

Vernon Paul Cherry

Scott Matthew Davidson

Leon Smith, Jr.

Peter Anthony Vega

Ladder 131

Christian Michael Otto
    Regenhard

Ladder 132

*Battalion Chief Thomas
    Theodore Haskell, Jr.

Andrew Jordan

Michael Kiefer

Thomas Mingione

John T. Vigiano II

Sergio Villanueva

Ladder 136

Michael Joseph Cawley

Ladder 148

Lt. Philip Scott Petti

Ladder 157

Lt. Stephen G. Harrell

Ladder 166

William X. Wren

Rescue 1

Capt. Terence S. Hatton

Lt. Dennis Mojica

Joseph Angelini, Sr.

Gary Geidel

William Henry

Kenneth Joseph Marino

Michael Montesi

Gerard Terence Nevins

Patrick J. O'Keefe

Brian Edward Sweeney

David M. Weiss

Rescue 2

Lt. Peter C. Martin

*Lt. John Napolitano

William David Lake

Daniel F. Libretti

Kevin O'Rourke

Lincoln Quappe

Edward Rall

Rescue 3

Christopher Joseph Blackwell

Thomas Foley

Thomas Gambino, Jr.

Raymond Meisenheimer

Donald J. Regan

Gerard Patrick Schrang

Joseph Spor

Rescue 4

*Battalion Chief Brian Hickey

Lt. Kevin Dowdell

Terrence Patrick Farrell

William J. Mahoney

Peter Allen Nelson

Durrell V. Pearsall

Rescue 5

*Battalion Chief Louis Joseph
Modafferi

Lt. Harvey Harrell

*Fire Marshal Andre G.
Fletcher

John P. Bergin

Carl Vincent Bini

Michael Curtis Fiore

Joseph Mascali

Douglas Charles Miller

Jeffrey Matthew Palazzo

Nicholas P. Rossomando

Allan Tarasiewicz

Special Operations

Battalion Chief John Moran

*Deputy Chief Raymond
Mathew Downey

*Deputy Chief Charles Kasper

*Deputy Chief John M.
Paolillo

Squad 1

*Chief James M. Amato

*Capt. Michael Esposito

Lt. Edward A. D'Atri

*Lt. David J. Fontana

Lt. Michael Thomas Russo,
Sr.

Gary Box

Thomas M. Butler

Peter Carroll

Matthew David Garvey

Stephen Gerard Siller

Squad 18

*Capt. William E. McGinn

*Lt. Andrew Fredericks

*Lt. David Halderman

Eric Allen

Timothy Haskell

Manuel Mojica

Lawrence Virgilio

Squad 41

Lt. Michael K. Healey

Thomas Patrick Cullen III

Robert Hamilton

Michael J. Lyons

Gregory Sikorsky

Richard Bruce Van Hine

Squad 252

Lt. Timothy Higgins

*Lt. Patrick Lyons

Tarel Coleman

Thomas Kuveikis

Peter J. Langone

Kevin Prior

Squad 288

*Lt. Ronnie E. Gies

Lt. Ronald T. Kerwin

Peter Brennan

Joseph Hunter

Jonathan Lee Ielpi

Adam David Rand

Timothy Matthew Welty

EMS Battalion 49

Paramedic Carlos R. Lillo

EMS Battalion 57

*EMS Lt. Ricardo J. Quinn

Safety Battalion 1

Chief Lawrence T. Stack

Robert Crawford

New York Fire Patrol

Keith M. Roma, Fire Patrol 2

DAD'S GUYS

New York City Police Department (NYPD)

Sgt. Timothy A. Roy, Sr.

Sgt. John Gerard Coughlin

Sgt. Rodney C. Gillis

Sgt. Michael S. Curtin

Det. Joseph V. Vigiano

Det. Claude Daniel Richards

Moira Ann Smith

Ramon Suarez

Paul Talty

Santos Valentin, Jr.

Walter E. Weaver

Ronald Philip Kloepfer

Thomas M. Langone

James Patrick Leahy

Brian Grady McDonnell

John William Perry

Glen Kerrin Pettit

John D'Allara

Vincent Danz

Jerome M. P. Dominguez

Stephen P. Driscoll

Mark Joseph Ellis

Robert Fazio, Jr.

228 | PARKER

MIKE'S GUYS

<u>Port Authority Police Department (PAPD)</u>

Supt. Ferdinand V. Morrone	Clinton Davis, Sr.
Chief James A. Romito	Donald A. Foreman
Lt. Robert D. Cirri	Gregg J. Froehner
Insp. Anthony P. Infante, Jr.	Uhuru Gonga Houston
Capt. Kathy Nancy Mazza	George G. Howard
Sgt. Robert M. Kaulfers	Thomas E. Gorman
Donald James McIntyre	Stephen Huczko, Jr.
Walter Arthur McNeil	Paul William Jurgens
Joseph Michael Navas	Liam Callahan
James Nelson	Paul Laszczynski
Alfonse J. Niedermeyer	David Prudencio Lemagne
James Wendell Parham	John Joseph Lennon, Jr.
Dominick A. Pezzulo	John Dennis Levi
Antonio J. Rodrigues	James Francis Lynch
Richard Rodriguez	John P. Skala
Bruce Albert Reynolds	Walwyn W. Stuart, Jr.
Christopher C. Amoroso	Kenneth F. Tietjen
Maurice V. Barry	Nathaniel Webb

Michael T. Wholey